HOW TO CODE

A STEP-BY-STEP GUIDE TO
COMPUTER CODING

Max Wainewright

QED

Quarto is the authority on a wide range of topics.

Quarto educates, entertains and enriches the lives of our readers—enthusiasts and lovers of hands-on living.

www.quartoknows.com

Publisher: Maxime Boucknooghe
Design and illustration: Mike Henson
Design: Angela and Dave Ball
Editor: Claudia Martin
Editorial Assistant: Harriet Stone
Consultant: Sean McManus
Editorial Director: Victoria Garrard
Art Director: Laura Roberts-Jensen

First published in the UK in 2016 by
QED Publishing
Part of The Quarto Group
The Old Brewery,
6 Blundell Street,
London, N7 9BH

ISBN 978 1 78493 665 5

Printed in China

Scratch is developed by the Lifelong Kindergarten Group at MIT Media Lab. See http://scratch.mit.edu

For more information on Logo:
www.logofoundation.org

CONTENTS

Here's how you can get hold of Logo, Scratch and Python so you can start experimenting.

LOGO

Logo was originally designed by Seymour Papert over 40 years ago. There are various versions of it available.

If you are using a PC, you can download a free version of Logo from: **www.softronix.com/logo.html**

Alternatively you can start using Logo straight away by opening up your web browser and visiting: **http://turtleacademy.com/playground/en** or **www.calormen.com/jslogo/**

SCRATCH

You can use Scratch on a PC or Mac by opening your web browser and going to: **http://scratch.mit.edu** – then click **'Create'** or **'Try it out'**.

There is a very similar website called Snap that also works on iPads. It is available here: **http://snap.berkeley.edu/run**

If you want to run Scratch without using the internet, you can download it from here: **http://scratch.mit.edu/scratch2download/**

INSTALLING PYTHON ON A PC

1. Go to: **www.python.org**.
2. Click **'Downloads'** then choose **'Download Python'** (version 3.4 or higher).
3. Double-click the downloaded file, then follow the instructions on screen.
4. Click the **'Start'** button, click **'Python'**, then click **'IDLE'**. (In Windows 8, go to the top right of the screen and click **'Search'**, then type in 'idle' and click the program to run it.)

INSTALLING PYTHON ON A MAC

1. Go to: **www.python.org**.
2. Click **'Downloads'** then choose **'Download Python'** (version 3.4 or higher).
3. Double-click the downloaded file, then follow the instructions on screen.
4. To start using Python quickly, click **'Spotlight'** Q (at the top right of the screen).
5. Type 'idle' Spotlight idle then press **'Enter'**.

Making an icon for Python on a Mac (this will make it easier to find):

1. Open **'Finder'**.
2. Under the **'Go'** menu, click on **'Applications'**.
3. Scroll down to **Python** and click on it.
4. Drag the **IDLE** icon to the 'dock' (menu bar) at the bottom or side of the screen.

Internet safety

Children should be supervised when using the internet, particularly when using an unfamiliar website for the first time.
The publisher and author cannot be held responsible for the content of the websites referred to in this book.

CONTENTS :: CHAPTER 1

Enter

INTRODUCTION

This book is going to teach you how to code – that's another way of saying that you'll learn how to tell computers what to do. First of all, let's meet our friendly robot Ada, who is named after the world's first computer programmer: Ada Lovelace.

Meet Ada

Ada Lovelace (1815–52) was born in England 200 years ago. She worked out that a machine would be able to solve problems if it was given step-by-step instructions – a program. However, there were no computers yet for her to test her ideas on!

What is coding?

Coding means writing a set of words, or 'code', that will tell a computer what to do. The words need to be written in a special language that the computer will understand. This chapter looks at two languages: Logo and Scratch. Coding is also called computer programming. All computers need a program to tell them what to do. Laptops, tablets, phones and desktop computers all need programs to be useful.

Inside your computer

Input

A mouse, keyboard and touch screen are all 'input devices'. They let us put information into a computer or tablet.

Input

Input

Input

Output

A printer, screen and speakers are all 'output devices'. Output devices are ways for a computer to tell you things.

Output

Output

Output

We work in the computer's memory. A computer needs memory to store information.

Programs are read from the memory and turned into simple coded instructions.

Welcome to the processor - the brain of the computer!

Input devices can be used to type in programs, or change what a program does.

Processor

We follow instructions - giving the user our results through output devices.

GIVING INSTRUCTIONS

There are lots of ways we can ask people to do things. If someone said 'turn on the lights', 'put the lights on' or even 'it's dark – turn on the thingy', you would know what to do. But to program a computer, we need to give exactly the right words – and in the right order. Words that tell computers and people what to do are called instructions.

Making breakfast

Imagine you are programming our friendly robot Ada to make breakfast. Can you put these instructions in the correct order?

A Open the cereal box.

B Pour some milk onto the cereal.

C Take the lid off the milk carton.

D Tip some cereal into the bowl.

E Get a bowl from the cupboard.

Become a human robot

It's time to become a human robot! It will help you think about how to give precise instructions. You need a partner to play this game.

One of you needs to pretend to be a robot. The other one needs to be the programmer and give instructions to the robot. This player's task is to give the robot instructions to walk to the door. The only commands that can be given to the robot are:

Walk forwards.

Turn left.

Turn right.

Stop.

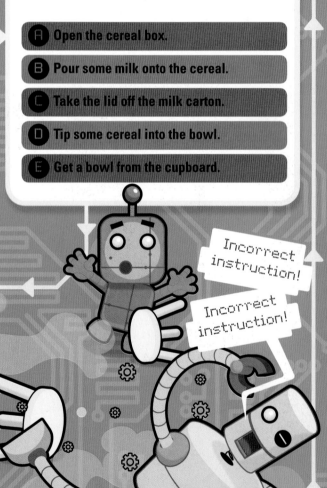

Incorrect instruction!

Incorrect instruction!

Robot artist

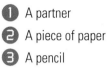

Here's another game to help you practise giving instructions.

You need:

1 A partner
2 A piece of paper
3 A pencil

Sit at a table next to your partner. One of you needs to be the robot artist, while the other is the programmer. The programmer needs to give the robot instructions to draw one of the pictures below. This time the robot is just moving a pencil. The robot partner is only allowed to do what the programmer says. Here are the commands you can use:

↑ Move up

Move left ◁   STOP!   ▷ Move right

↓ Move down

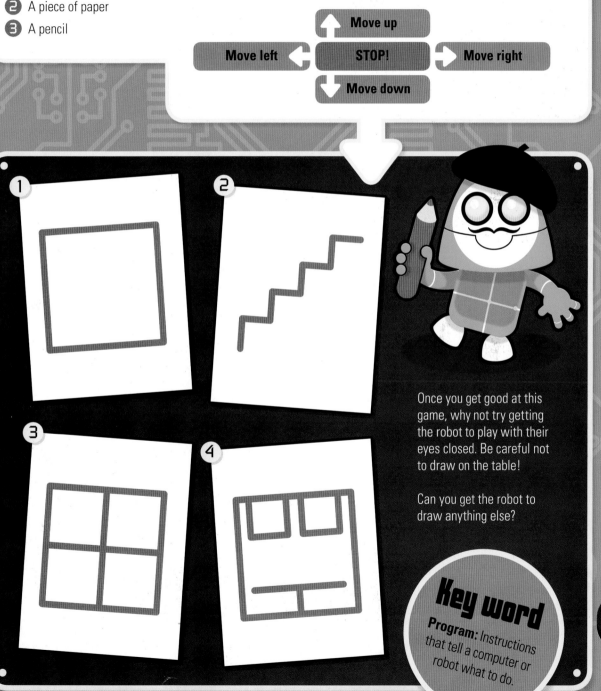

Once you get good at this game, why not try getting the robot to play with their eyes closed. Be careful not to draw on the table!

Can you get the robot to draw anything else?

Key word

Program: Instructions that tell a computer or robot what to do.

STEP BY STEP

Computer programs need instructions to make things happen. Sometimes we need a program to solve a particular problem. To solve that problem, we need to plan the steps the program will need to take – we call the steps an algorithm.

Take a journey

Here is your problem: Ada needs to travel from square number 3 to square number 4. Work out the steps she will need to take.

To travel from **3** to **4** Ada needs to take the following steps:

⬆ UP → ➡ RIGHT → ⬆ UP → ➡ RIGHT → ➡ RIGHT → ⬇ DOWN → ➡ RIGHT

Using the grid opposite, start at **1** and take the following steps. Where do you end up? Turn to page 32 for the answer.

⬇ DOWN → ⬇ DOWN → ⬇ DOWN → ⬇ DOWN → ⬇ DOWN → LEFT ⬅

If you like, you could write down letters instead of drawing arrows. For example, you could write **right, right, up, down** as **R R U D**.

1. Write down an algorithm that explains how to get from **6** to **1**
2. Now try to get from **5** to **6**
3. Travel from **2** to **4**

Now check your answers on page 32.

Key word

Algorithm: The steps a program needs to take in order to solve a problem.

1. R U U
2.

Amazing algorithms game

For this game, you'll just need a dice and a counter. Have a try:

1. Throw the dice once. Put your counter on the number you threw.
2. Throw the dice again (if you get the same number, throw again).
3. This is the number you need to get to.
4. Write down the steps you need to take to get there.

Use a coin or a toy person as a counter.

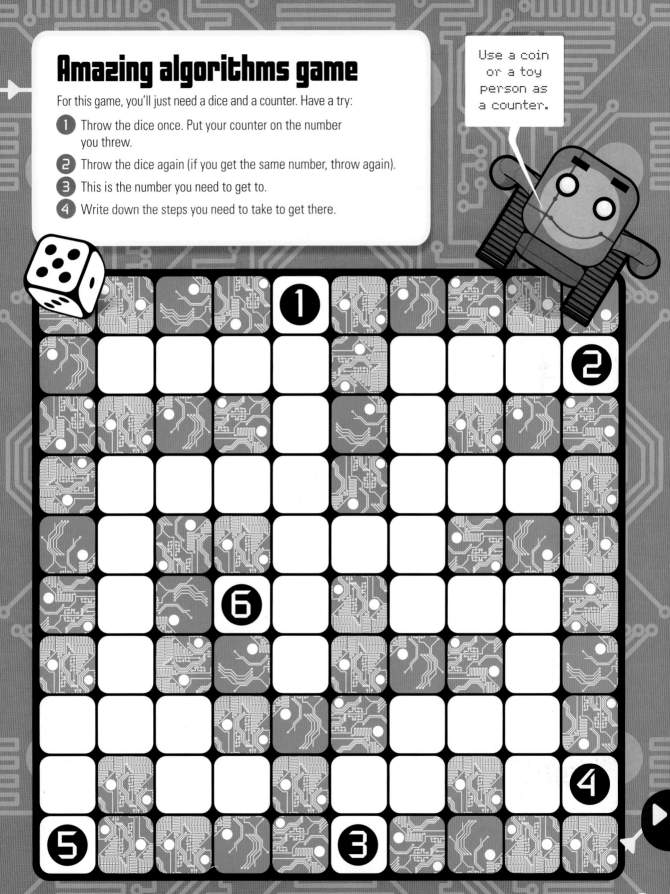

CODED MESSAGES

Giving commands

R5 means move right 5 squares. The red blob tells you where to start.

We're going to make our instructions more useful by using numbers to show how far we need to move in each direction. Special instructions like this are called commands.

Example commands

U4 means: Move up 4.
L3 means: Move left 3.
D7 means: Move down 7.
R4 means: Move right 4.

Let's see what **R3 U3 L3 D3** will draw. You need to start at the red blob:

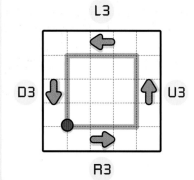

L3

D3   U3

R3

Oops! That was too far.

Word game

Now have a go at writing down the commands that will spell out these words:

There's more than one right answer for some of these!

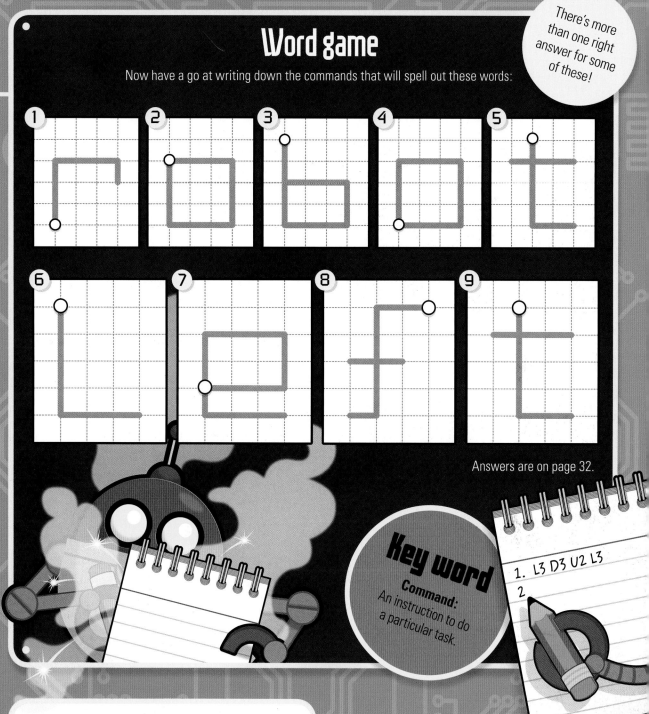

Answers are on page 32.

Key word

Command:
An instruction to do a particular task.

1. L3 D3 U2 L3
2

You name it!

Try to write down the commands to spell out your name or initials. You'll need squared paper and a pencil.

1. Draw your name on squared paper. You'll have to turn diagonals (like in V, W or M) into horizontal and vertical lines!

2. Write down the commands to draw your letters.

3. Give the commands to a partner to see if they can follow them.

SPINNING AROUND

Get to grips with degrees

The amount that robots turn is measured in degrees. Degrees can be hard to understand, but getting to grips with the basics will allow you to make your robot make turns. A right angle is 90 degrees. A complete turn around is 360 degrees. Basically, the bigger the number, the bigger the turn.

Now we're going to learn how to make a robot move around. We need to use three commands: move forward, turn left or turn right – and by how much.

Degrees are measured from 0 to 360. A turn of 360 degrees makes a full circle.

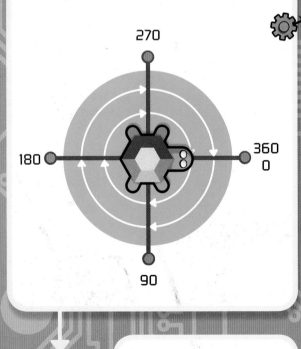

Here are examples of simple commands to make your robot turn right and left:

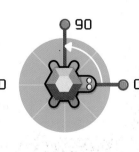

Turn right 90   Turn left 90

Tell it to turn

We're going to try this program:

Forward 25
Right 90
Forward 20
Right 90
Forward 25
Left 90
Forward 10

If you're having trouble working out lefts and rights, try turning this page around to face the same way as the turtle.

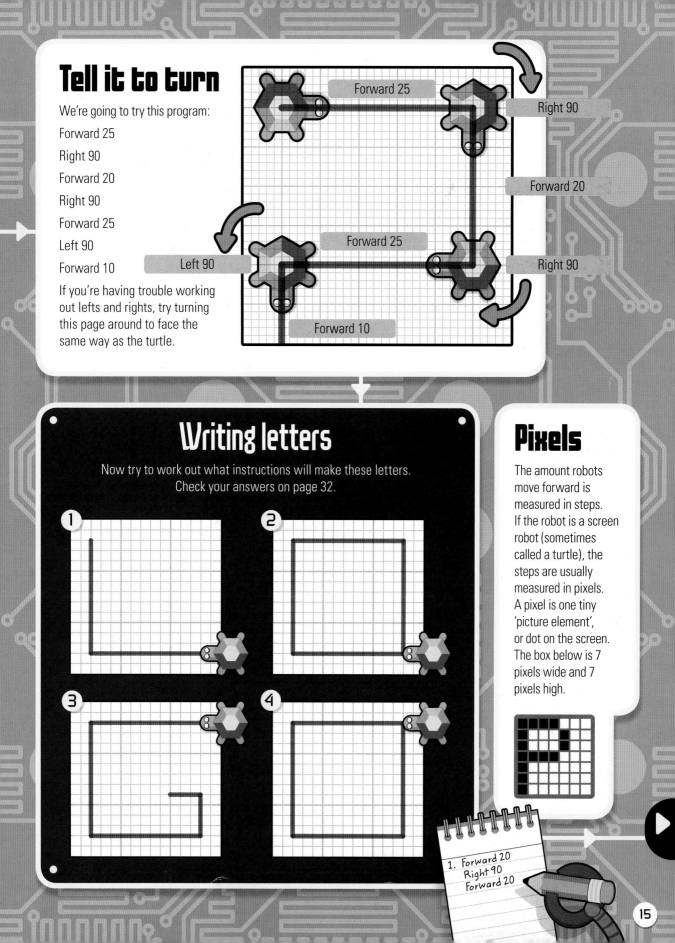

Forward 25
Right 90
Forward 20
Forward 25
Left 90
Right 90
Forward 10

Writing letters

Now try to work out what instructions will make these letters.
Check your answers on page 32.

1
2
3
4

Pixels

The amount robots move forward is measured in steps. If the robot is a screen robot (sometimes called a turtle), the steps are usually measured in pixels. A pixel is one tiny 'picture element', or dot on the screen. The box below is 7 pixels wide and 7 pixels high.

1. Forward 20
   Right 90
   Forward 20

LEARNING LOGO

We're going to learn how to program in Logo, which is one of the simplest computer languages. Using Logo is a great way to put some basic commands into action!

The Logo screen

Before we start learning some commands, let's look at what we will see on the Logo screen. In the example below, we've already typed three commands into the command box. You can press **'Enter'** after each command – or type a series of commands separated by spaces, then press **'Enter'** to see the result.

This is the drawing box.

Each version of Logo is slightly different. Some have **'Run'** buttons and some don't.
If your version doesn't, then press **'Enter'** after typing a command.

If there is only a thin command box, type commands one at a time, then press **'Enter'**, or click **'Run'** to run them one at a time. Alternatively, type several commands in a line with a space between each command, then press **'Enter'** or click **'Run'** to test them all.

This is the command box. Type your program here.

Click **'Run'** to test your code or press the **'Enter'** key.

Turn to page 4 for help with downloading Logo or finding a website where you can use it.

fd 50
rt 90
fd 50

Run

```
fd = forward
rt = right
lt = left
```

Basic commands

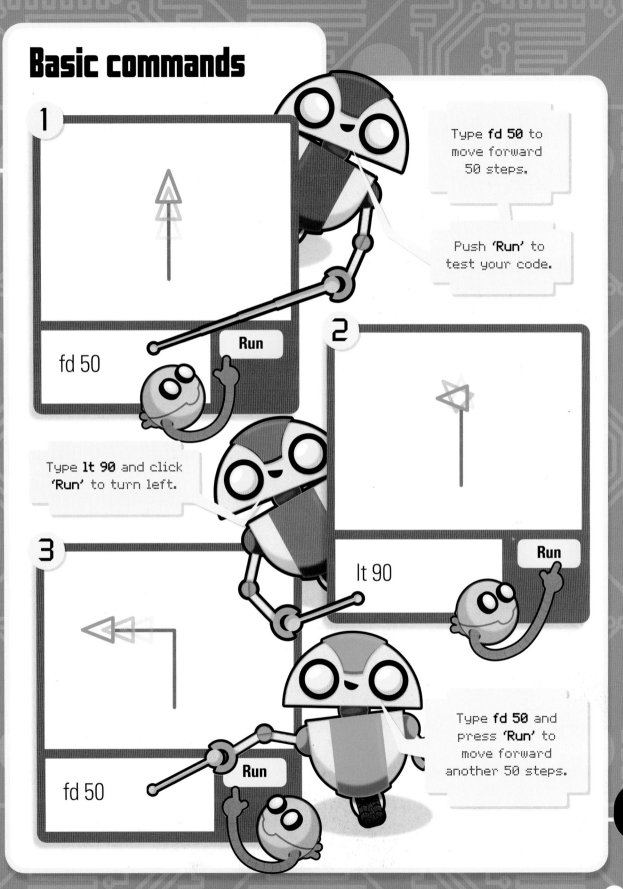

1

fd 50

Run

Type **fd 50** to move forward 50 steps.

Push **'Run'** to test your code.

2

lt 90

Run

Type **lt 90** and click **'Run'** to turn left.

3

fd 50

Run

Type **fd 50** and press **'Run'** to move forward another 50 steps.

LOGO SHAPES

Get in shape

Type in these programs to practise coding with Logo:

```
fd 60
rt 90
fd 60
rt 90
fd 60
rt 90
fd 60
```

Now you understand how Logo works, have a go at drawing different shapes. Experiment with what you can create – now you're doing some clever coding!

Type **cs** when you need to clear the screen.

```
fd 50
lt 90
fd 100
lt 90
fd 50
lt 90
fd 100
```

```
fd 100
rt 90
fd 50
lt 90
lt 90
fd 100
```

```
fd 25
rt 90
fd 25
lt 90
fd 25
rt 90
fd 25
```

lt 90 means turn left 90 degrees.

Type **seth 0** to make the turtle point up again.

Now spend some time experimenting. See what you can draw with Logo!

18

Try these

What do these programs draw?

1
```
lt 90
fd 50
rt 90
fd 100
rt 90
fd 50
```

2
```
fd 100
rt 90
fd 100
rt 90
fd 100
rt 90
fd 100
```

3
```
fd 50
rt 90
fd 50
lt 90
fd 50
rt 90
fd 50
rt 90
fd 100
rt 90
fd 100
```

Super Computer 7000

Shape up!

Now try to draw these shapes using Logo:

4

5

6

7

Amazing!

Ooooo!

Aaahh!

See page 32 for suggested answers.
There is more than one right answer!

STARTING SCRATCH

Move 20 steps

Scratch uses a similar approach to Logo, making a turtle (or sprite) move around the screen.

The Scratch screen

First of all, let's get used to the basic idea of how Scratch works. In Scratch you drag and join your commands together instead of typing them. Start by going to the Scratch website.

For help finding Scratch and similar programs turn to page 4.

Click **'Create'** or **'Try it out'**. Your screen should look like the one below.

TRY IT OUT

Choose the group of commands from here.

File▼ Edit▼ Tips About

Scripts   Costumes   Sounds

Motion   Events
Looks   Control
Sound   Sensing
Pen   Operators
Data   More Blocks

Move 10 steps

Turn 15 degrees

Turn 15 degrees

Pen down
Move 10 steps
Turn 10 degre
Move 80 steps

I am the sprite that obeys your commands.

This area is called the stage. This is where you can watch your sprite moving about.

These are the commands in the current group.

This is the scripts area – drag your commands over here. If you need to remove a command, just drag it off the scripts area.

How to make a simple program

1 Choose the **Motion** group of commands. Drag a '**Move 10 steps**' command block to the scripts area.

Move 10 steps

Turn ↻ 15 degrees

Turn ↺ 15 degrees

Move 10 steps

2 Click it!

On the stage, the cat sprite should move 10 steps.

Move 10 steps

Turn ↻ 15 degrees

Turn ↺ 15 degrees

Move 10 steps

3 Change your code to '**Move 20 steps**', by clicking in the box and typing '20'.

Click it to test it.

Move 20 steps

4 Drag a '**Turn 15 degrees**' code block to join it.

Click to test your code.

Move 20 steps

Turn ↻ 15 degrees

Experiment by changing the amount to move and turn.

5 You can drag several code blocks together to make a program!

Move 20 steps

Turn ↻ 15 degrees

Move 80 steps

Turn ↺ 15 degrees

Click any block to run the whole program.

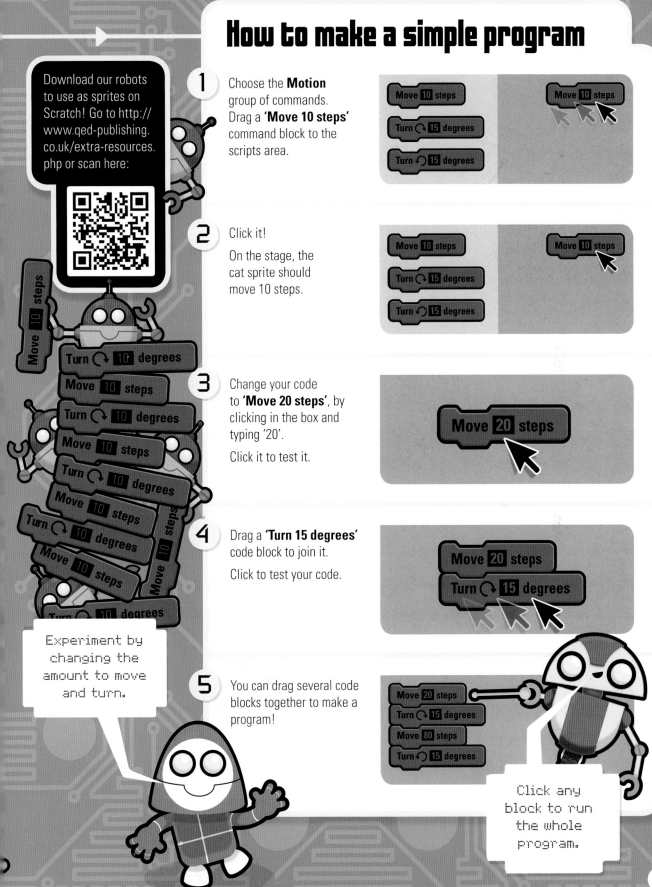

21

PEN DOWN

Now let's learn how to draw using Scratch. We need to use the command 'Pen down', then command the sprite to move around.

All square

Try this exercise to draw a square:

1 Click on the **Pen** group.

Looks	Control
Sound	Sensing
Pen	Operators
Data	More Blocks

2 Drag '**Pen down**' to the scripts area.

Pen down   Pen down

3 Click on the **Motion** group.

Motion	Events
Looks	Control
Sound	Sensing

4 Drag a '**Move 10 steps**' code block to join on to your program.

Move **10** steps   Pen down
                          Move **10** steps

5 Change the 10 to 60.

Pen down
Move **60** steps

6 Complete the program:

Pen down
Move **60** steps
Turn ↻ **90** degrees
Move **60** steps
Turn ↻ **90** degrees
Move **60** steps
Turn ↻ **90** degrees
Move **60** steps

Click any block to run the program.

22

Drawing shapes

Now change your code so it looks like this:

```
Pen down
Move 20 steps
Turn ↻ 90 degrees
Move 80 steps
Turn ↻ 90 degrees
Move 20 steps
Turn ↻ 90 degrees
Move 80 steps
```

Try to guess what your code will draw. Then click the first command to run your code.

Do not panic!
Do not PANIC!!

Turn   degrees   n down   steps
Pen down   Move 10 steps
degrees   turn 10 degrees

Storing your work

Click the **File** menu at the top of the screen on the left. Then click:
New – to start some new work.
Download to your computer – to save a file on to your computer.
Upload from your computer – to open a file you have saved earlier.

More shapes!

Now try to draw these shapes using Scratch:

① ② ③ ④

See page 33 for answers.

PRESS A KEY

So far, all the code we have written runs when we tell it to start. We are now going to learn how to make our code change when different keys are pressed. A key press during a program is a type of input.

Right and left

When **'R'** is pressed, we want the sprite to move right. When **'L'** is pressed, we want it to move left.

Press R to move right

①
Browser
scratch.mit.edu

Start Scratch. Click **'Create'** or **'Try it out'**.

②
Scripts　Costumes　Sounds

Motion　　Events
Looks　　　Control
Sound　　　Sensing
Pen　　　　Operators
Data　　　More Blocks

Click on the **Events** group.

③
when space▼ key pressed

Drag **'When key pressed'** to the scripts area.

④
when space▼ key pressed

p
q
r
s

Select **'r'** as your key.

⑤
Scripts　Costumes　Sounds

Motion　　Events
Looks　　　Control
Sound　　　Sensing
Pen　　　　Operators
Data　　　More Blocks

Click on the **Motion** group.

⑥
when r▼ key pressed
move 10 steps

Drag **'Move steps'** to the scripts area.

Now try pressing the **R** key on the keyboard...

Press L to move left

1

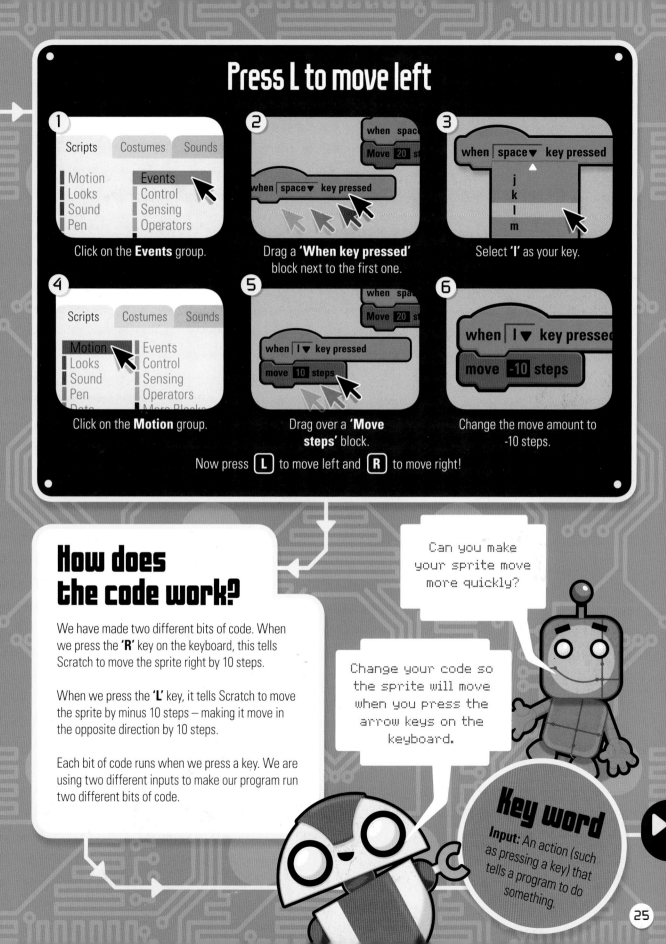

Scripts	Costumes	Sounds
Motion	Events	
Looks	Control	
Sound	Sensing	
Pen	Operators	

Click on the **Events** group.

2

when space
Move 20 st

when space▾ key pressed

Drag a **'When key pressed'** block next to the first one.

3

when space▾ key pressed

j
k
l
m

Select **'l'** as your key.

4

Scripts	Costumes	Sounds
Motion	Events	
Looks	Control	
Sound	Sensing	
Pen	Operators	

Click on the **Motion** group.

5

when spa
Move 20 st

when l▾ key pressed

move 10 steps

Drag over a **'Move steps'** block.

6

when l▾ key pressed

move -10 steps

Change the move amount to -10 steps.

Now press **L** to move left and **R** to move right!

How does the code work?

We have made two different bits of code. When we press the **'R'** key on the keyboard, this tells Scratch to move the sprite right by 10 steps.

When we press the **'L'** key, it tells Scratch to move the sprite by minus 10 steps – making it move in the opposite direction by 10 steps.

Each bit of code runs when we press a key. We are using two different inputs to make our program run two different bits of code.

Can you make your sprite move more quickly?

Change your code so the sprite will move when you press the arrow keys on the keyboard.

Key word

Input: An action (such as pressing a key) that tells a program to do something.

INPUTS AND DIRECTIONS

We've learnt how to move a sprite to the right and left. We will now find out how to move it up, down and any other direction you want by pressing different keys.

Using degrees to make turns

We are going to make a program that has four different input keys. Each input key will run code that makes the sprite point in a different direction.

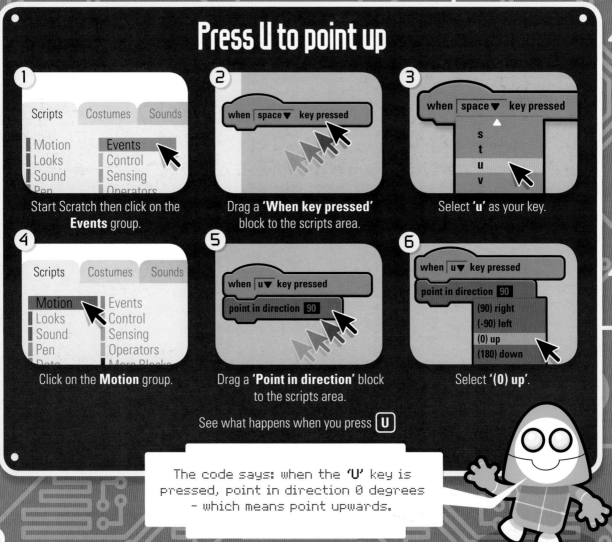

Press U to point up

1
Scripts | Costumes | Sounds
Motion | Events
Looks | Control
Sound | Sensing
Pen | Operators

Start Scratch then click on the **Events** group.

2
when space ▼ key pressed

Drag a **'When key pressed'** block to the scripts area.

3
when space ▼ key pressed
s
t
u
v

Select **'u'** as your key.

4
Scripts | Costumes | Sounds
Motion | Events
Looks | Control
Sound | Sensing
Pen | Operators
Data | More Blocks

Click on the **Motion** group.

5
when u ▼ key pressed
point in direction 90

Drag a **'Point in direction'** block to the scripts area.

6
when u ▼ key pressed
point in direction 90
(90) right
(-90) left
(0) up
(180) down

Select **'(0) up'**.

See what happens when you press **U**

The code says: when the 'U' key is pressed, point in direction 0 degrees – which means point upwards.

Press D to point down

We still need to make the sprite move. When we press 'D', we want it to point down.

1

```
when u▼ key pressed
point in direction 0
move 10 steps
```

Drag in a **'Move steps'** block. Press **U** to test it!

2

```
when space▼ key pressed
Move 20 st

when space▼ key pressed
```

Drag over another **'When key pressed'** block. Put it next to the first one.

3

```
when space▼ key pressed
b
c
d
e
```

This time, select **'d'** as your key.

4

```
when d▼ key pressed
point in direction 90
```

Drag in a **'Point in direction'** block.

5

```
when d▼ key pressed
point in direction 90
(90) right
(-90) left
(0) up
(180) down
```

Select **'(180) down'**.

6

```
when d▼ key pressed
point in direction 180
move 10 steps
```

Drag in another **'Move steps'** block.

Check your code works by pressing **U** and **D**

You need to finish this program by adding code to make the sprite move left and right. Add two more **'When key pressed'** blocks, so they change the sprite's direction when **'L'** and **'R'** are pressed.

Point **left** and move:

```
when l▼ key pressed
point in direction -90
move 10 steps
```

Point **right** and move:

```
when r▼ key pressed
point in direction 90
move 10 steps
```

Woohoo!

SKETCHING WITH INPUTS

Now that we know how to move a sprite around with input commands, we are going to make a simple sketching program. Players will be able to draw what they want by pressing different keys to paint up, down, left or right.

Create your own drawing game

1

Start Scratch, then make a program that will move the sprite up, down, left and right. Turn back to page 26 for a reminder of how to do this.

Test your program!

```
when [u ▼] key pressed
point in direction 0
move 10 steps

when [l ▼] key pressed
point in direction -90
move 10 steps

when [r ▼] key pressed
point in direction 90
move 10 steps

when [d ▼] key pressed
point in direction 180
move 10 steps
```

Challenge

Try changing the keys used to move things around. You could use the cursor (arrow) keys.

2

We need to make the sprite draw a line when it moves. Click on the **Pen** group. Drag a **'Pen down'** block onto the scripts area. Click the **'Pen down'** block, then try pressing the **U**, **D**, **R** and **L** keys.

| Looks |
| Sound |
| Pen |
| Data |

Pen down

3

To clear the screen we need to use the **'Clear'** command block. Drag it over to the scripts area then try clicking it.

| Looks |
| Sound |
| Pen |
| Data |

Clear

4

Join the **'Clear'** and **'Pen down'** blocks together.

Click on the **Events** group. Drag over a **'When green flag clicked'** block and put it above the **'Clear'** and **'Pen down'** blocks.

Now the sprite will be ready to draw a new picture whenever the green flag is clicked.

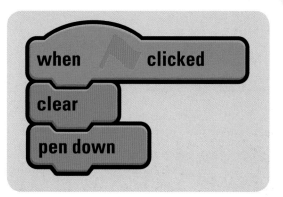

```
when [flag] clicked
clear
pen down
```

5

The large sprite can get in the way when drawing.

Shrink it using this icon. ⟩⟨

Click the icon then click on the sprite to make it smaller.

Scripts

Your program is now complete! Click the green flag icon to start using it to draw.

Computers use numbers to represent colours. Scratch uses numbers between 0 and 199. Some other languages use up to 16 million different colours!

Do you like my new jumper? I wanted something that was coloured a bit 15,999,999!

Challenge

Can you add some commands that will let players change the pen colour? You will need to use **'When key pressed'** blocks from the **Events** group, and **'Set pen colour to'** blocks from the **Pen** group.

```
when [g ▼] key pressed
set pen colour to [50]
```

You will need to add a **'When key pressed'** block and **'Set pen colour to'** block for each colour you want to use. Experiment with different numbers and keep testing your code.

DEBUGGING

Coding can be a process of trial and error – testing out ideas and seeing if they work. It is quite usual to make mistakes when doing this. A bug is another name for a mistake in a piece of code that stops it working properly. Debugging means fixing those mistakes. You'll find the answers to these questions on page 33.

1 Bugs for breakfast

Get started with debugging by finding the mistake in these instructions for making a piece of toast:

1 Get a piece of bread.

2 Put it in the toaster.

3 Spread butter on the toast.

4 Take the toast out of the toaster.

2 B wrong

Here are some commands to draw a letter b, like the one shown here. But what's wrong with the commands?

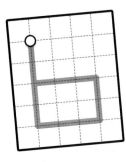

Start at the blob.
D4 R3 D2 L3

3 Logo bug

This rectangle is 100 pixels high and 300 pixels wide.

300

100

This code should draw the rectangle – but there's a bug or two somewhere!

```
fd 100
rt 90
fd 300
rightt 90
fd 100
rt 90
fd 90
```

Scratch bug

Here is some Scratch code to draw a square. The square should be 200 pixels by 200 pixels.

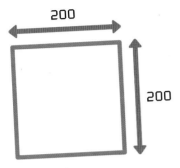

200

200

Find the bug in the code:

```
Pen down
Move 200 steps
Turn ↻ 90 degrees
Move 200 steps
Turn ↻ 90 degrees
Move 200 steps
Turn ↻ 90 degrees
Move 200 steps
```

Key word

Debugging: Getting rid of mistakes that stop your code from working properly.

Broken game

This Scratch program should make a sprite do two things:

Move **up** when **U** is pressed.

Move **down** when **D** is pressed.

Find the bug in the code.

```
when u ▼ key pressed
point in direction 0
move 10 steps
```

```
when d ▼ key pressed
point in direction 90
move 10 steps
```

Here are some tips to help you when you're debugging.

Debugging tips

When your code doesn't do what you want it to:

1. Go through your code step by step, thinking about what each command does.
2. Draw a picture or diagram to help you.
3. Have a break for a few minutes!

Think about these guidelines when you are coding:

1. Plan your program carefully first, either with a diagram or some written notes.
2. When you are learning to code, it is better to write lots of small, simple programs rather than one larger and more complex program.
3. Test your program as you are building it – don't wait until you have put in all the commands.

Page 10

You end up at square 6.

1 R U U U U U

2 U U R U U U U R R D D L

3 L L L D D D D R R D D D R

Page 13

1 U3 R3 D1

2 R3 D3 L3 U3 or D3 R3 U3 L3

3 D4 R3 U2 L3 or D2 R3 D2 L3 U2

4 U3 R3 D3 L3 or R3 U3 L3 D3

5 D1 L1 R3 L2 D3 R2 or D1 R2 L3 R1 D3 R2

6 D4 R3

7 R3 U2 L3 D3 R3 or U2 R3 D2 L3 D1 R3

8 L2 D2 L1 R2 L1 D2 L1 or L2 D2 R1 L2 R1 D2 L1

9 D1 L1 R3 L2 D3 R2 or D1 R2 L3 R1 D3 R2

Page 19

1
2
3

4 fd 100
rt 90
fd 100
rt 90
fd 100
rt 90
fd 100
rt 180
fd 50
lt 90
fd 100

5 fd 80
lt 90
fd 40
rt 90
fd 20
rt 90
fd 100
rt 90
fd 20
rt 90
fd 40
lt 90
fd 80
rt 90
fd 20

6 fd 100
rt 90
fd 100
rt 90
fd 100
rt 90
fd 100
rt 90
fd 50
rt 90
fd 100
rt 90
fd 50
rt 90
fd 50
rt 90
fd 100

7 fd 30
rt 90
fd 30
lt 90
fd 30
rt 90
fd 30
lt 90
fd 30
rt 90
fd 30
lt 90
fd 30
rt 90
fd 30
lt 90
fd 30
rt 90
fd 120
rt 90
fd 120

Page 15

1 forward 11
right 90
forward 11

2 forward 11
right 90
forward 11
right 90
forward 11
right 90
forward 11

3 forward 11
left 90
forward 11
left 90
forward 11
left 90
forward 4
left 90
forward 3

4 forward 11
left 90
forward 11
left 90
forward 11
left 90
forward 11

Happy programming!
See you in chapter 2.

Page 23

There are hundreds of ways these could be solved –
here are some examples:

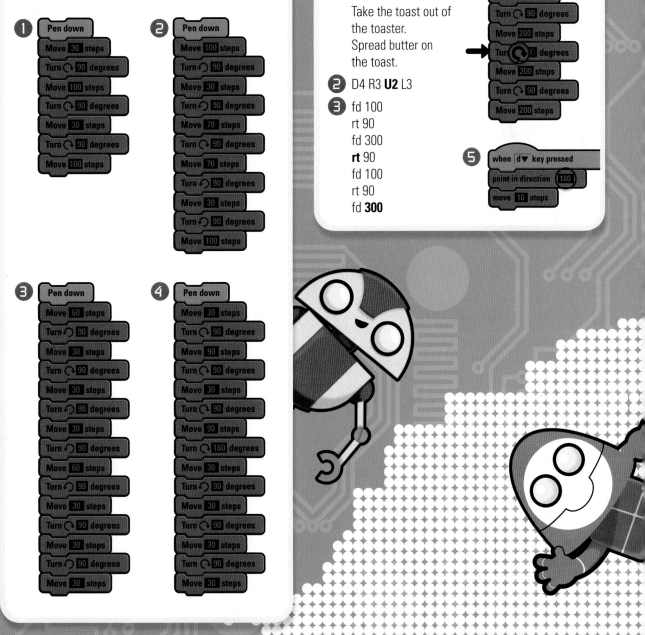

1
Pen down
Move 30 steps
Turn ↻ 90 degrees
Move 100 steps
Turn ↻ 90 degrees
Move 30 steps
Turn ↻ 90 degrees
Move 100 steps

2
Pen down
Move 100 steps
Turn ↺ 90 degrees
Move 30 steps
Turn ↺ 90 degrees
Move 70 steps
Turn ↻ 90 degrees
Move 70 steps
Turn ↺ 90 degrees
Move 30 steps
Turn ↺ 90 degrees
Move 100 steps

3
Pen down
Move 60 steps
Turn ↺ 90 degrees
Move 30 steps
Turn ↻ 90 degrees
Move 30 steps
Turn ↺ 90 degrees
Move 30 steps
Turn ↺ 90 degrees
Move 60 steps
Turn ↺ 90 degrees
Move 30 steps
Turn ↻ 90 degrees
Move 30 steps
Turn ↺ 90 degrees
Move 30 steps

4
Pen down
Move 30 steps
Turn ↻ 90 degrees
Move 90 steps
Turn ↻ 90 degrees
Move 30 steps
Turn ↻ 90 degrees
Move 90 steps
Turn ↻ 180 degrees
Move 30 steps
Turn ↺ 90 degrees
Move 30 steps
Turn ↻ 90 degrees
Move 30 steps
Turn ↻ 90 degrees
Move 30 steps

Pages 30–31

1 Get a piece of bread.
Put it in the toaster.
Take the toast out of
the toaster.
Spread butter on
the toast.

2 D4 R3 **U2** L3

3 fd 100
rt 90
fd 300
rt 90
fd 100
rt 90
fd **300**

4
Pen down
Move 200 steps
Turn ↻ 90 degrees
Move 200 steps
Turn ↻ 90 degrees
Move 200 steps
Turn ↻ 90 degrees
Move 200 steps

5
when d▼ key pressed
point in direction 180
move 10 steps

CONTENTS :: CHAPTER 2

Enter

INTRODUCTION

This chapter will show you how to become better at coding by learning how to use loops, sound and variables. We're going to use two simple and free-to-use programming languages: Logo and Scratch. For help with downloading them or finding a website where you can use them, turn to page 4. But first let's have a quick reminder about how to start coding.

What is coding?

Coding means writing a set of words or numbers that will tell a computer what to do. Coding is also called computer programming. To program a computer, we need to use the right words in the correct order.

Let's see what these instructions – or commands – will draw: **U3 R2 D2 R2**.

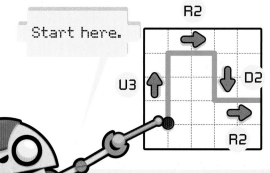

Start here.

U3 means move up 3 squares. **R2** means move right 2.

fd 60 makes the turtle move forwards 60 steps.

fd **30**
rt **90**
fd **60**
rt **90**
fd **30**
rt **90**
fd **60**

Using Logo, we can practise simple programming – like commanding the computer to draw a rectangle. **Fd 90** means 'move forward 90 steps'. **Rt 90** means 'turn right by 90 degrees' – that's a quarter turn to the right, making a right angle.

Scratch uses a similar approach to Logo, making a sprite move around the 'stage' area in the top left of the Scratch screen. But with Scratch, you drag and join your commands rather than typing them.

This is the scripts area – drag your commands over here. If you need to remove a command, drag it off the scripts area.

This area is called the stage.

Choose the group of commands from here.

What are loops, outputs and variables?

In the next few pages, we'll learn how to use loops to make programs repeat things over and over.

repeat 5 [draw_square]

Making a sprite or turtle move or draw is just one possible output. An output is information that a computer produces, as a result of commands we give it. In this chapter, we will find out how to code another output – sound.

When e ▼ key pressed

play note 64 ▼ for 0.5 beats

Finally we'll explore variables. Variables are a way that computer programs store pieces of data (information).

Age = 8

Q W E R

AGE

Key word

Code: A set of special words or blocks that tells a computer what to do.

LOOPS

Computers are very good at doing things over and over again. A loop is a way of making your program do something repetitive – like count up to 20, draw a shape with lots of sides, or make a spaceship orbit round and round a planet.

Why use loops?

Imagine you want to write a program to draw a square. You could do it like this:

1. **Draw the first side.**
2. **Turn 90 degrees.**
3. **Draw the second side.**
4. **Turn 90 degrees.**
5. **Draw the third side.**
6. **Turn 90 degrees.**
7. **Draw the fourth side.**
8. **Turn 90 degrees.**

It would take 8 separate instructions. A loop makes this much simpler. With a loop we just need 3 instructions:

1. **Repeat this 4 times:**
2. **Draw a side.**
3. **Turn 90 degrees.**

There must be a better way to do this!

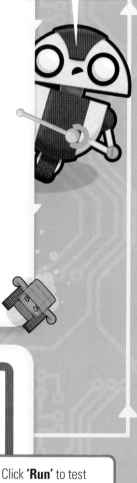

Logo loops

We're going to write some Logo programs to try out making repeat loops. First of all, in case you're new to Logo, let's get to grips with how to use it.

This is the drawing box. The output of your program will show up here.

Click **'Run'** to test your code or press the **'Enter'** key.

This is your command box. Type your program here.

```
fd 50 rt 90 fd 50
```

Run

Coding simple loops

Try typing this code into the Logo command box, then press **'Return'** or click **'Run'**.

| repeat 4 [fd 50 rt 90] | **Run** |

How many times to repeat the commands.

Any commands between the square brackets get repeated.

Key word

Loop: A set of repeated instructions.

| repeat 4 [fd 50 rt 90] | **Run** |

You have drawn a square using a loop!

Now try changing the commands inside the square brackets and experimenting with the number of times to repeat the commands. Here are some examples to get you started. What shapes do these loops draw?

1. | repeat 8 [fd 50 rt 45] | **Run** |
2. | repeat 6 [fd 50 rt 60] | **Run** |
3. | repeat 3 [fd 50 rt 120] | **Run** |
4. | repeat 3 [fd 100 rt 120] | **Run** |
5. | repeat 5 [fd 100 rt 72] | **Run** |
6. | repeat 36 [fd 10 rt 10] | **Run** |
7. | repeat 4 [fd 100 lt 90] | **Run** |
8. | repeat 20 [fd 10] | **Run** |

Check the answers on page 62.

Type **cs** or reload the webpage after each question to clear the screen.

Loops in everyday life

We use loops in everyday life without thinking about it. When your teacher hands out books, he or she says, 'Hand out all the books,' not, 'Hand out this book, then this book, then this book...' and so on! Your parents say, 'Eat up all your peas!' not, 'Eat that pea, then that one, then that one...!' We use words like 'each' or 'every' to give our everyday commands – it's the same as saying 'repeat 20' in a loop.

Happy birthday! Blow out each candle!

PATTERNS WITH LOOPS

In Logo, we can combine repeat loops to make patterns. We'll learn how to use just a couple of commands to make Logo perform hundreds of instructions. In Logo, measurements are made in pixels – the tiniest dots that you can see on your screen.

Practise patterns

Type the following commands to draw a small square:

```
repeat 4 [ fd 20 rt 90 ]
```
Run

Now draw 8 of those squares in a line using another repeat command wrapped around the first repeat command:

```
repeat 8 [ repeat 4 [ fd 20 rt 90 ] fd 25 ]
```
Run

This works because the code tells Logo:

Repeat this 8 times:
Draw a square, then move forward a bit.

This time we are going to draw 36 squares using repeat commands, but turn a small angle (10 degrees) after drawing each square:

```
repeat 36 [ repeat 4 [ fd 50 rt 90 ] rt 10 ]
```
Run

You should see a pattern like this:

You should see a pattern like this.

Now try changing your code slightly to see how the pattern changes. Experiment with different values for the size of the square, and the number of times it gets repeated.

You can also use **setpc** (set pen colour) and a number to change the colour of the pattern: e.g. **setpc 5.**

How does the pattern work?

When one loop runs inside another loop like this, they are called nested loops.

repeat 4 [fd 50 rt 90]

The inner loop draws one square.

repeat 36 [rt 10]

The outer loop repeats it 36 times, then turns right by 10 degrees.

1

Now try combining three patterns on top of each other. We'll start with a large square with a side of 120 pixels.

```
repeat 36 [ repeat 4 [ fd 120 rt 90 ] rt 10 ]   Run
```

2

Now change the colour to red:

```
setpc 4   Run
```

Next we are going to draw another pattern on top of the first one, with a shorter side length of 80 pixels:

```
repeat 36 [ repeat 4 [ fd 80 rt 90 ] rt 10 ]   Run
```

3

Now change the colour to blue:

```
setpc 1   Run
```

Finish off with a smaller square side of 60 pixels:

```
repeat 36 [ repeat 4 [ fd 60 rt 90 ] rt 10 ]   Run
```

Key word

Pixel: A tiny 'picture element' – or dot on the computer screen.

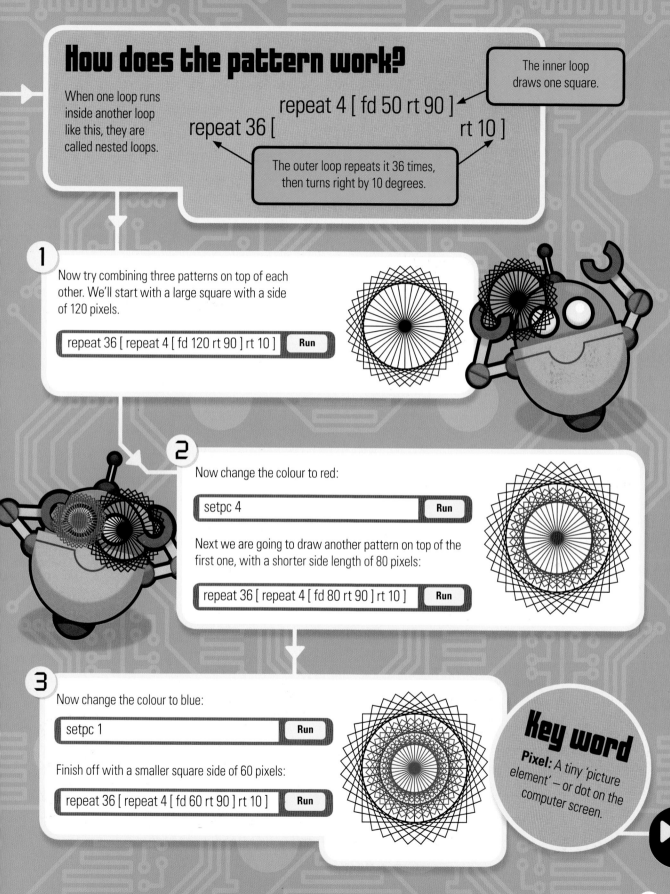

LOOPS IN SCRATCH

Now we're going to look at how we can use loops in Scratch. Loops work the same way in Scratch as in Logo, but instead of typing your commands, you drag and drop them. Let's have a go.

Draw a square

If you wanted to draw a square in Logo, you would type:

`repeat 4 [ fd 10 rt 90 ]` **Run**

In Scratch, we can create the same code by dragging **'Repeat'**, **'Move'** and **'Turn'** blocks:

1 Go to the Scratch website then click **'Create'** or **'Try it out'**. Turn to page 4 for help. Now click on the **'Scripts'** tab in the centre of the Scratch screen. Choose the **Control** group.

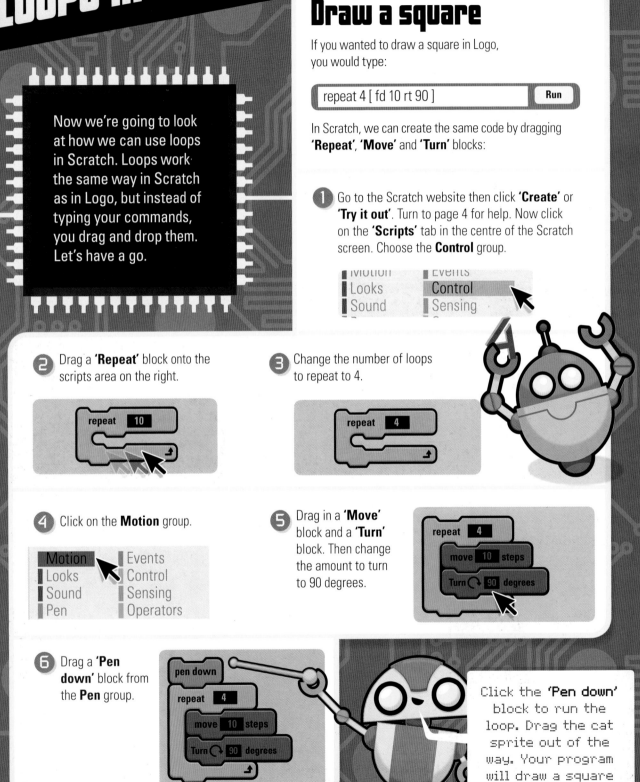

Motion	Events
Looks	Control
Sound	Sensing

2 Drag a **'Repeat'** block onto the scripts area on the right.

repeat 10

3 Change the number of loops to repeat to 4.

repeat 4

4 Click on the **Motion** group.

Motion	Events
Looks	Control
Sound	Sensing
Pen	Operators

5 Drag in a **'Move'** block and a **'Turn'** block. Then change the amount to turn to 90 degrees.

repeat 4
move 10 steps
Turn ↻ 90 degrees

6 Drag a **'Pen down'** block from the **Pen** group.

pen down
repeat 4
move 10 steps
Turn ↻ 90 degrees

Click the **'Pen down'** block to run the loop. Drag the cat sprite out of the way. Your program will draw a square on the screen.

Saving your work

Click the **'File'** menu at the top of the page on the left. Then click:
New – to start some new work.
Download to your computer – to save a file on to your computer.
Upload from your computer – to open a file you have saved earlier.

Practising Scratch loops

Create these 5 loop blocks on the scripts area. You'll also need to drag over a **'Pen down'** and a **'Clear'** block. Try clicking on the **'Pen down'** code block and then on each of the **'Repeat'** blocks in turn. Click **'Clear'** to erase your shapes. Test out what each of the loops draws. Check the answers on page 62.

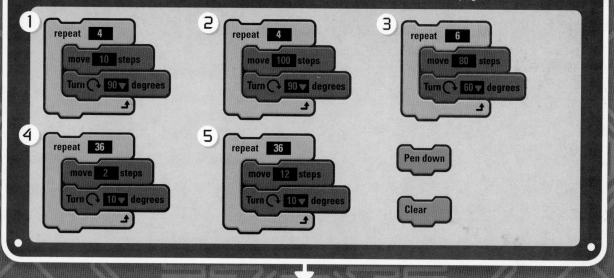

1. repeat 4
   move 10 steps
   Turn 90 degrees

2. repeat 4
   move 100 steps
   Turn 90 degrees

3. repeat 6
   move 80 steps
   Turn 60 degrees

4. repeat 36
   move 2 steps
   Turn 10 degrees

5. repeat 36
   move 12 steps
   Turn 10 degrees

Pen down

Clear

After drawing each of the shapes above, try dragging the Scratch sprite to a new space on the screen. You can start building up a picture or pattern.

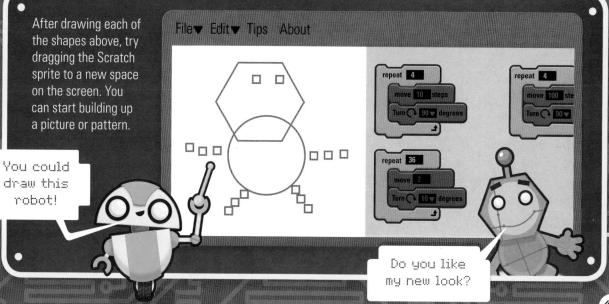

File▼ Edit▼ Tips About

repeat 4
move 10 steps
Turn 90 degrees

repeat 4
move 100 ste
Turn 90

repeat 36
move 2
Turn 10 degrees

You could draw this robot!

Do you like my new look?

LOOPS FOREVER

How to code a swimming fish

1 Start by going to the Scratch website. Delete the main sprite by right-clicking on it and then choosing **'Delete'**.

Sometimes we need loops that run forever. This is particularly useful in games where we want something to keep happening, like moving a sprite around. We're going to code a game where a fish keeps swimming around the screen, following the mouse pointer.

Right-clicking means press this button if you're on a PC. If you're on a Mac, press **'Control'** and click.

2 Now make your own fish sprite. Start by clicking **'Paint new sprite'**.

Select the **Ellipse** tool.

Set to fill in.

Choose orange.

Draw a wide ellipse.

Draw more ellipses... and use the **Erase** or **Select** tool to delete the back of its tail.

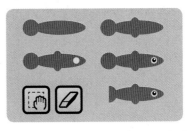

3 Now click on the **'Scripts'** tab next to the red stop button. You're going to drag some code to the scripts area to make the fish swim forward once the program starts.

Drag the **'When green flag clicked'** block from the **Events** group.

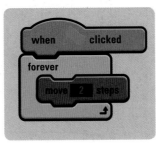

Drag the **'Forever'** loop block from the **Control** group and the **'Move'** block from the **Motion** group.

Change the **'Move...steps'** value to 2 to slow the fish down.

Click the green flag (near the top of the screen) to test your code.

4

To make the fish change direction, drag the **'Point towards'** block from the **Motion** group into the loop. Set it to 'mouse pointer'.

Test your code by clicking the green flag!

Every time the loop repeats, it makes the fish point towards the mouse pointer. It also moves it every loop. Without loops, the game wouldn't work!

5

Now draw your own background picture for the game.

First click **'Stage'**.   Then click **'Backdrops'**.

Click the **Fill** tool and choose a blue colour. Now click the background to colour it in.

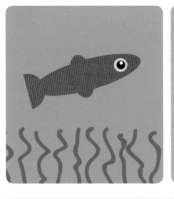

Use the **Brush** tool to draw some reeds.

Use the **Line width** slider to change the size of the reeds.

Your program is now complete! Click the green flag icon at the top of the screen to start playing.

REPEAT UNTIL...

Sometimes we need to stop loops when something happens – for example, if a player in a game bumps into a wall. To program things like this, we use a 'repeat until' loop. We are going to code a simple maze game to learn how to use this technique.

How to code a maze game

1

Start Scratch. Drag code to the scripts area to make the Scratch sprite move slowly across the screen, pointing towards the mouse pointer.

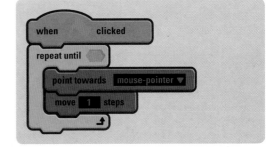

For help, see steps 3 and 4 on pages 44–45. But use a **'Repeat until'** block instead of a **'Forever'** block.

Change the speed of the sprite to move 1 step each loop.

2

Make the Scratch sprite smaller by clicking the **Shrink** icon at the top of the screen, and then clicking the Scratch sprite several times.

3

To make the sprite start in the same place each time, drag the **'Set x to'** and **'Set y to'** code blocks from the **Motion** group to the scripts area.

Experiment with changing the **'Set x'** and **'Set y'** values.

Ow!

Click the green flag to test your code.

Set x and y coordinates

`set x to -200`

'Set x to' tells Scratch how far to place the sprite to the left or right of the screen.

`set y to 100`

'Set y to' tells Scratch how far to place the sprite up or down the screen.

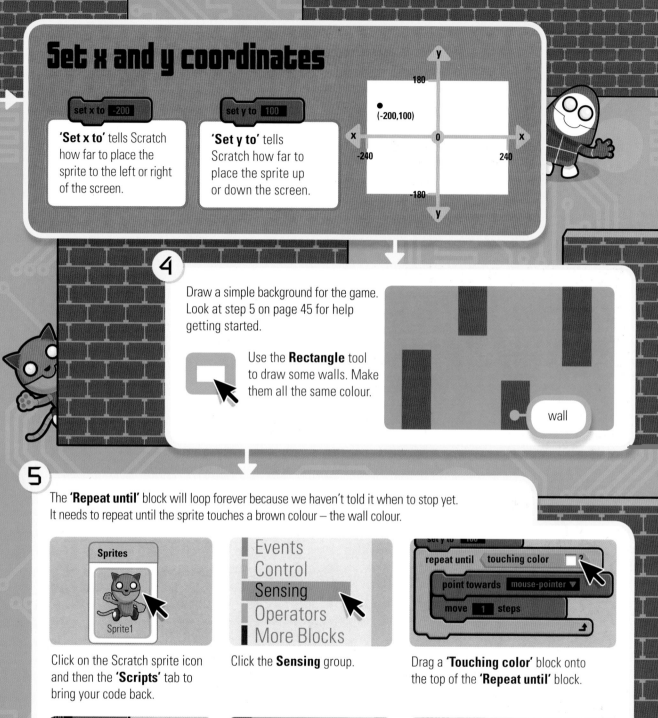

(-200,100)

y
180

x -240

x 240

0

-180

y

④

Draw a simple background for the game. Look at step 5 on page 45 for help getting started.

Use the **Rectangle** tool to draw some walls. Make them all the same colour.

wall

⑤

The **'Repeat until'** block will loop forever because we haven't told it when to stop yet. It needs to repeat until the sprite touches a brown colour – the wall colour.

Sprites

Sprite1

Click on the Scratch sprite icon and then the **'Scripts'** tab to bring your code back.

Events
Control
Sensing
Operators
More Blocks

Click the **Sensing** group.

`repeat until < touching color ☐ ?`
`point towards mouse-pointer ▼`
`move 1 steps`

Drag a **'Touching color'** block onto the top of the **'Repeat until'** block.

Click the coloured square then choose the colour to check for...

...by clicking one of the walls.

`repeat until < touching color ☐ ?`

Now your game will play until the sprite hits a wall. Test it by clicking the green flag at the top of the screen. To play again, drag your sprite away from the wall.

REPEAT UNTIL CAUGHT

Eeeeek!

We're going to practise using 'repeat until' loops by creating another game. This will have two sprite objects, the Scratch cat sprite and a dog, which will chase after the cat. The player will control the cat, moving it around the screen until it is caught.

1

How to code a chase game

Drag code to the scripts area to make the Scratch sprite move slowly across the screen, pointing towards the mouse pointer.

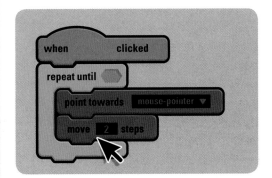

Look at steps 3 and 4 on pages 44–45 for help. Remember to use the **'Repeat until'** loop. Change the speed of the sprite to move 2 steps each loop.

2

Make the Scratch sprite smaller by clicking the **Shrink** icon at the top of the screen, and then clicking the Scratch sprite several times.

Click the green flag at the top of the screen to test your code.

3

Pick me!

Now add the second sprite.

Click this icon to choose a new sprite from the library.

Dog1   Dog2

Then scroll down to the **dog** and click on it.

OK Click **'OK'**.

 Use the **Shrink** icon to make the dog smaller.

Pick me!

Pick me!

Pick me!

4

Now we will make the dog sprite move.

Sprites

Sprite1   Dog2

Click the **dog** so the code you are about to build will control the dog rather than the cat!

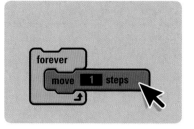

```
forever
  move  1  steps
```

Drag in a **'Forever'** loop block from the **Control** group. Add a **'Move'** block. Set it to 1 step each loop.

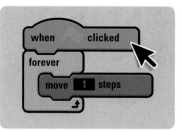

```
when      clicked
forever
  move  1  steps
```

From the **Events** group, drag a **'When green flag clicked'** block over. Put it at the top of the code.

5

After step 4, test your code. The cat should follow the mouse pointer. The dog should move in a straight line forever - this means it might get stuck on the right side of the screen. Just drag it to the left!

To make the dog chase the cat, click the **dog** sprite.

Sprites

Sprite1   Dog2

From the **Motion** group, drag on a **'Point towards'** code block. Set it to 'Sprite1'.

```
when      clicked
forever
  move  1  steps
  point towards  Sprite1 ▾
                 mouse-pointer
                 Sprite1
```

6

Now the most important part — making the 'until' part of the 'repeat until' loop! The aim is to keep the cat moving until the dog catches it.

Sprites

Sprite1   Dog2

Click the **cat** sprite.

Now click the green flag and start to play your game!

```
when      clicked
repeat until  touching  ▾ ?
                        mouse-pointer
  point towards  mous   edge
  move  2  steps        Dog2
```

Drag a **'Touching'** code block from the top of the **Sensing** group and set it to 'Dog2'.

ADDING SOUND

Our code so far has used two different inputs: pressing keys and moving the mouse. Our outputs have all been on screen. We are now going to learn how to control another sort of output – sound.

Getting started with sound in Scratch

Click the **Sound** group.

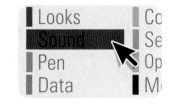

Drag a **'Play note'** code block onto the scripts area and try clicking it.

Key word

Output: The information produced by a computer, such as sound or movements of the sprite.

Changing beats

Try changing the value in the 'beats' box to 2. Click the code block.

Now change it to a small number – 0.25 (a quarter of a beat). Click it.

The bigger the number, the longer the note is played. Experiment!

Changing the note

Change how high or low the note is by changing the value in the 'note' box.

Either type a number in, or choose a note from the keyboard.

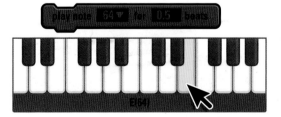

The higher the number, the higher the note. The lower the number, the lower the note.

You may not be able to hear notes much below 20, or above 100 – but your dog might!

Creating a tune

Drag a few **'Play note'** code blocks onto the scripts area and change their note values.

Click the top one to play all the notes. Experiment to make your own tune!

play note **64 ▼** for **0.5** beats
play note **62 ▼** for **0.5** beats
play note **60 ▼** for **0.5** beats
play note **60 ▼** for **0.5** beats

Make a piano program

1 Click the **Events** group.

Events
Control

2 Drag a **'When key pressed'** code block onto the scripts area and set it to 'q'.

When **q ▼** key pressed
o
p
q
r ▼

3 Click the **Sound** group.

Motion   Eve
Looks   Cor
Sound   Ser
Pen   Ope
Data   M

4 Drag a **'Play note'** code block onto the **'When key pressed'** code block, so the note will be played when the 'q' key is pressed.

When **q ▼** key pressed
play note **60 ▼** for **0.5** beats

5 Repeat steps 1 to 4 to create more blocks of code. Then change the value of the keys that they will respond to, and the notes they will play, so they look like this:

When **q ▼** key pressed
play note **60 ▼** for **0.5** beats

When **w ▼** key pressed
play note **62 ▼** for **0.5** beats

When **e ▼** key pressed
play note **64 ▼** for **0.5** beats

Add more **'When key pressed'** blocks to complete your piano. You can experiment with the **'Set instrument'** block to change the sound.

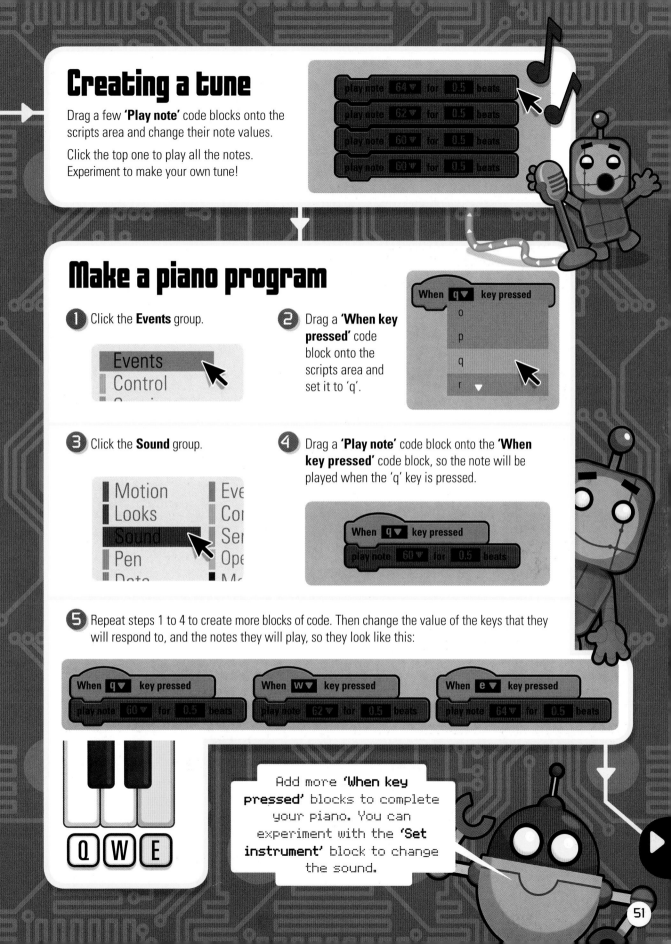

51

SOUND EFFECTS

The previous pages looked at how we could make sound using code. We are now going to look at how we can use sound within loops, and how to add sound effects to games.

Create a drum machine

We can combine sound effects with loops to make a simple drum machine.

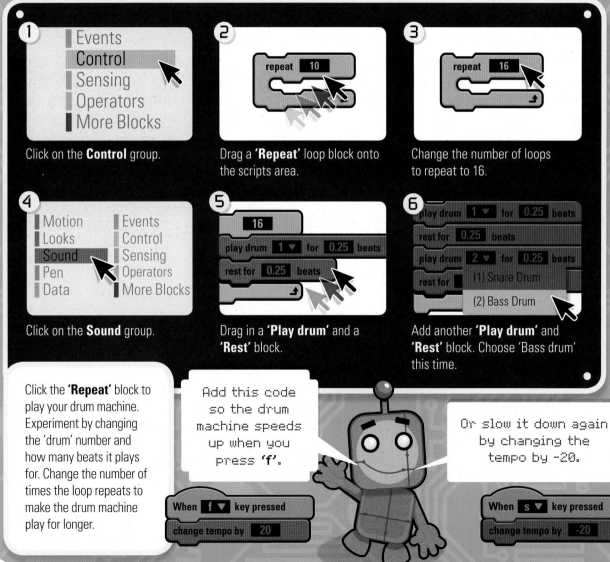

1 Click on the **Control** group.

2 Drag a **'Repeat'** loop block onto the scripts area.

3 Change the number of loops to repeat to 16.

4 Click on the **Sound** group.

5 Drag in a **'Play drum'** and a **'Rest'** block.

6 Add another **'Play drum'** and **'Rest'** block. Choose 'Bass drum' this time.

(1) Snare Drum

(2) Bass Drum

Click the **'Repeat'** block to play your drum machine. Experiment by changing the 'drum' number and how many beats it plays for. Change the number of times the loop repeats to make the drum machine play for longer.

Add this code so the drum machine speeds up when you press **'f'**.

Or slow it down again by changing the tempo by -20.

When **f ▼** key pressed
change tempo by **20**

When **s ▼** key pressed
change tempo by **-20**

Add sound to your games

Games can be a lot more fun if they have sound effects. We are going to learn how to add sound to the games we made in the previous pages.

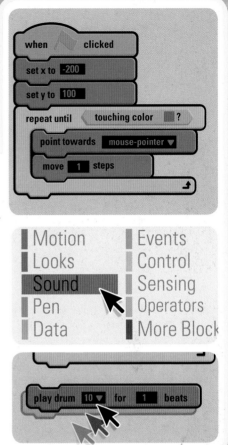

1 Make the **Maze Game** on page 46.

We are going to add a sound effect that is played when the player crashes into a wall.

We need to work out where to put a **'Play drum'** code block.

It needs to be put at the end of the **'Repeat until'** loop, outside the loop.

2 Click on the **Sound** group.

3 Drag a **'Play drum'** code block to the end of the loop and join it on.

Choose 'Drum 10' then test your game!

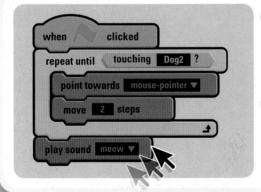

1 Make the **Chasing Game** on page 48.

Start by remaking the code for the cat and the dog. Check the game works properly first.

2 First, click on your **cat** sprite. From the **Sound** group, drag a **'Play sound meow'** code block to the end of the **'Repeat until'** loop for your cat sprite.

Now when the dog catches the cat, it will say 'meow'!

You can insert a start-up tune for your game here. Copy the one shown on the right – or compose your own!

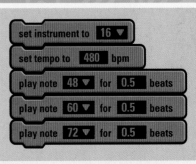

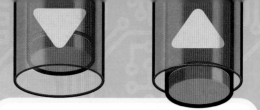

VARIABLES

Variables are a way that computer programs store pieces of data or information. They can be used to store things like your name, the score in a game or how big a shape is. Unlike normal numbers, variables can change their value when something happens.

Storing something in a variable

Most computer programming languages store values in variables in a similar way:

```
set age = 8
or
age = 8
```

They tell the computer that it needs to store the value 8 in a special box called 'age'.

A variable is a bit like a special box...

...that has something important stored inside.

What can variables be used for?

After a program has stored a value in a variable, it can be used by another part of the program. One part of the program might show the value of the variable to the person using it – as when the score is shown during a game. Or the program might do something if the value of a variable reaches a certain number – such as say, "Well done!"

AGE

SCORE

Ah! The score is 100. Time to stop the game – I'm off for a byte to eat!

Using variables in Scratch

Key word
Variable: A way that computer programs store information.

1

Click on the **Data** group.

Sound	Sensing
Pen	Operators
Data	More Bloc

2

Click **'Make a Variable'**.

Data   More B.

Make a Variable

3

Give the variable the name 'a'. Then click **'OK'**.

New Variable

Variable name: **a**

⦿ For all sprites   ◯ For this

OK

4

Drag the **'Change a by 1'** code block to the scripts area.

change a ▼ by 1

5

Click on the code block you dragged in. You should see the value of the variable change in the top left corner of the stage.

a   1

change a ▼ by 1

Keep clicking and it should keep going up!

PLES

AGE   SCORE   ENERGY   HAIR

Challenge

Try putting a **'Change a by 1'** code block inside a **'Repeat'** loop to make your variable count up to 20... or 100... or 500!

1...2...3... 4...5...6... 98...99...100

KEEPING SCORE

How to code a deadly shark game

1

Start Scratch. Delete the main sprite and create your own fish sprite.

Shrink the fish.

For help, see steps 1 and 2 on page 44.

We are going to make another chasing game, this time with the player avoiding a shark for as long as possible. We will use a variable to count how long the player avoids the shark, and use this variable as the score.

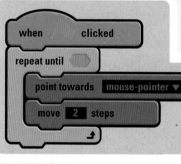

Sprite1

2

We will create code to make the fish swim towards the mouse pointer.

See pages 44–45 for help – but remember to use a **'Repeat until'** loop instead of a **'Forever'** loop.

Change the amount moved to 2 steps.

Click the green flag to test your code.

```
when [green flag] clicked
repeat until
    point towards  mouse-pointer ▼
    move  2  steps
```

3

w sprite:

Choose a colour and select the **Ellipse** tool. Draw a narrow ellipse.

Start to make a shark to chase the fish by clicking **'Paint new sprite'**.

Use lines to draw fins, nose and tail.

Then fill them in.

Add an eye.

If you make a mistake, use the **Undo** button.

Use the **Shrink** button to make the shark sprite smaller.

4

Now we will make a variable to keep the score.

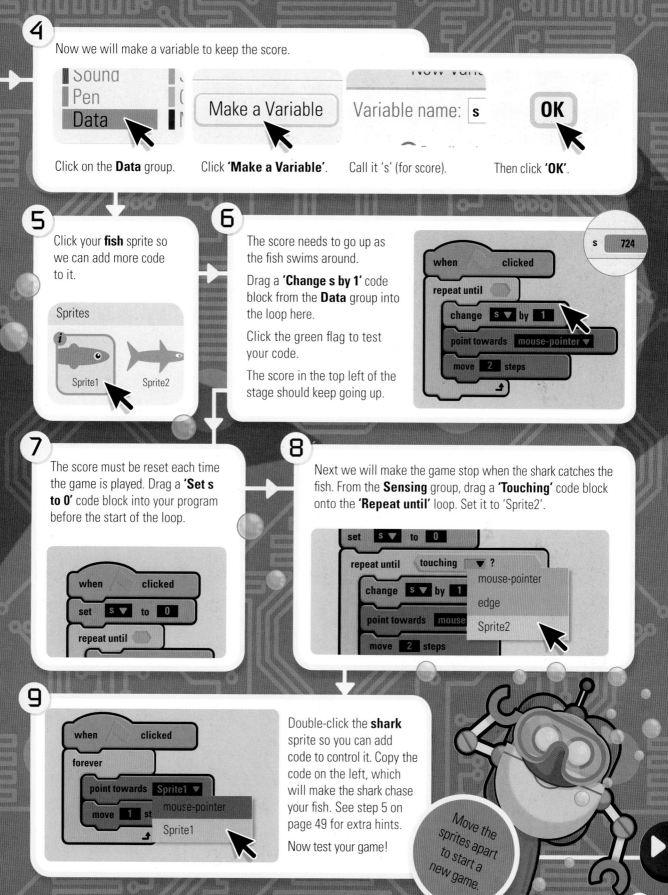

Click on the **Data** group.

Click **'Make a Variable'**.

Call it 's' (for score).

Then click **'OK'**.

5

Click your **fish** sprite so we can add more code to it.

Sprites

Sprite1   Sprite2

6

The score needs to go up as the fish swims around.

Drag a **'Change s by 1'** code block from the **Data** group into the loop here.

Click the green flag to test your code.

The score in the top left of the stage should keep going up.

s   724

when   clicked
repeat until
    change s ▼ by 1
    point towards mouse-pointer ▼
    move 2 steps

7

The score must be reset each time the game is played. Drag a **'Set s to 0'** code block into your program before the start of the loop.

when   clicked
set s ▼ to 0
repeat until

8

Next we will make the game stop when the shark catches the fish. From the **Sensing** group, drag a **'Touching'** code block onto the **'Repeat until'** loop. Set it to 'Sprite2'.

set s ▼ to 0
repeat until   touching   ▼ ?
    change s ▼ by 1   mouse-pointer
    point towards mouse   edge
    move 2 steps   Sprite2

9

when   clicked
forever
    point towards Sprite1 ▼
    move 1 st   mouse-pointer
                   Sprite1

Double-click the **shark** sprite so you can add code to control it. Copy the code on the left, which will make the shark chase your fish. See step 5 on page 49 for extra hints.

Now test your game!

Move the sprites apart to start a new game.

57

COUNTING CLICKS

Now we're going to learn how to use a variable to count mouse clicks. We will make a game where the player has to pat the cat as it moves across the screen. We need a variable to count the number of times the cat is patted. At the end of the game, the score will be shown.

Pat me if you can!

How to code a pat the cat game

1

Make a variable to keep the score.

Sound
Pen
Data

Make a Variable

New Varie...

Variable name: s

OK

Click on the **Data** group.

Click **'Make a Variable'**.

Call it 's' (for score).

Then click **'OK'**.

2

We will create a loop to move the cat. From the **Events** group, drag the **'When green flag clicked'** block. Drag a **'Repeat until'** block from the **Control** group and a **'Move'** block from the **Motion** group.

Change the **'Move...steps'** value to 5 to slow down the cat.

when clicked
repeat until
move 5 steps

3

The score must go up when the cat is clicked.

Click on the **Events** group. Drag the **'When this sprite clicked'** block to the scripts area.

Click on the **Data** group. Drag the **'Change s by 1'** code block to join it.

When this sprite clicked
change s by 1

s 7

Shrink the cat sprite and then test your code.

4

To make the cat start in the same place each time, we need to click on the **Motion** group.

Drag over a **'Set x to'** code block and drop it before the loop starts.

Set the 'x' value to -180.

See page 46 if you need help using 'Set x to'.

5

Every time we play the game, the score needs to go back to 0.

We need to add code telling Scratch to **'Set s to 0'** when the green flag is clicked to start the game.

Motion
Looks
Sound
Pen
Data

Click the **Data** group.

Drag on a **'Set s to 0'** block.

6

Next we will make the cat stop at the screen edge.

Control
Sensing
Operators
More Blocks

Click on the **Sensing** group.

Drag a **'Touching'** code block onto the **'Repeat until'** loop – and click 'edge'.

7

Finally, we would like to display the score at the end of the game.

Motion
Looks
Sound

Click on the **Looks** group.

Drag a **'Say...'** code block to the end of the **'Repeat until'** loop.

Sound
Pen
Data

Click on the **Data** group.

Drag the **'s'** code block onto the **'Say...'** block to display the score.

Click this button to make the game larger.

Challenge

Can you add sound effects to your game?
Make the cat say 'meow' every time you click it.

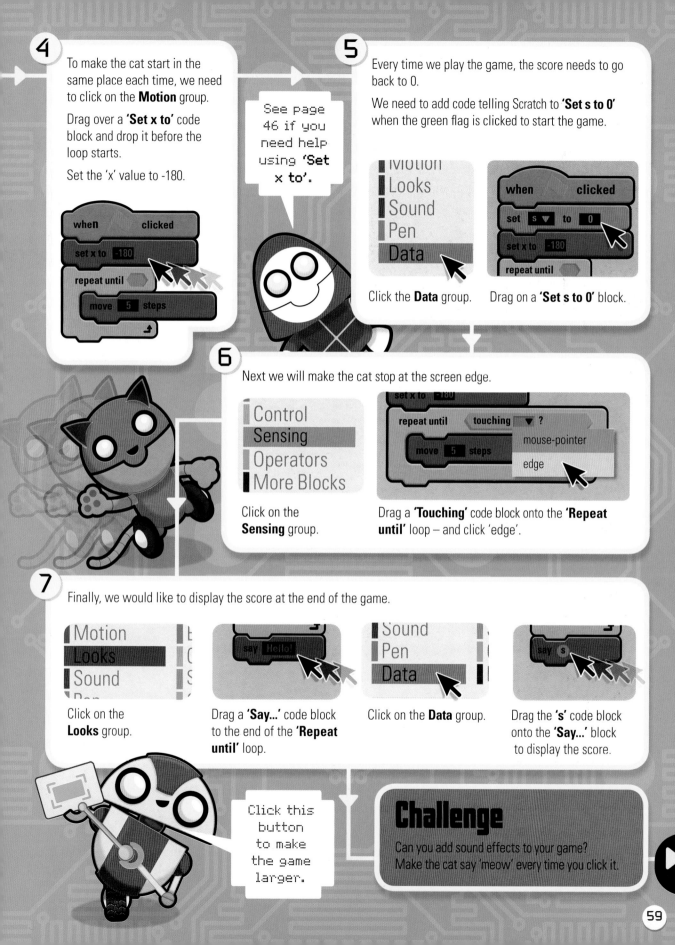

DEBUGGING

Coding can be a process of trial and error – testing ideas and seeing if they work. It is normal to make mistakes! A bug is another name for a mistake in a piece of code that stops it from working properly. Debugging means fixing those mistakes. Try these debugging exercises and find answers on page 62.

Key word

Debugging: Getting rid of mistakes that stop your code from working properly.

1 Debug this Logo code so it draws a square using a repeat loop.

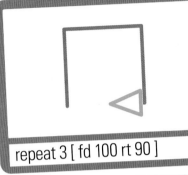

`repeat 3 [ fd 100 rt 90 ]`

2 Now fix this Logo code so it draws a square, too.

`repeat 4 [ fd 30 ] rt 90`

Debugging tips

When your code doesn't do what you want it to:

1 Work through your code step by step, thinking about what each command does.

2 Draw a picture or diagram to help.

3 Have a break for a few minutes!

3 This Scratch code has a bug in it. Fix it so it draws a square.

```
pen down
move 10 steps
repeat 4
    turn ↻ 90 degrees
```

4 The cat should stop when it hits a wall – but it doesn't! Find the bug.

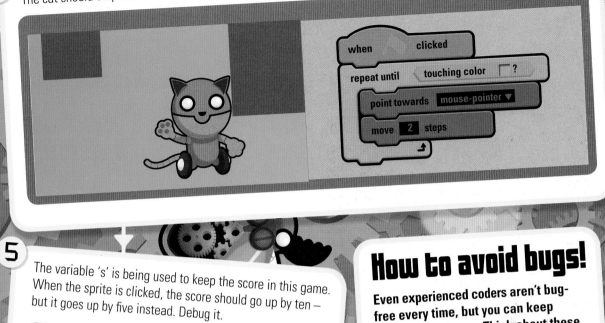

```
when        clicked
repeat until        touching color    ?
    point towards    mouse-pointer ▼
    move   2   steps
```

5 The variable 's' is being used to keep the score in this game. When the sprite is clicked, the score should go up by ten – but it goes up by five instead. Debug it.

```
s    15
```

```
When this sprite clicked
change  s ▼  by  5
```

How to avoid bugs!

Even experienced coders aren't bug-free every time, but you can keep bugs to a minimum. Think about these guidelines when you are coding:

1 Plan your program carefully, either with a diagram or some notes.

2 When you are learning to code, it is better to write lots of small, simple programs than one larger, complex program.

3 Test your program as you build it!

6 At the start of this game, the score (variable 's') should be set to 0. Every time the Scratch sprite is clicked, the score should go up by 1. Debug this code.

```
s    0
```

```
When this sprite clicked
set  s ▼  to  0
```

```
when        clicked
change  s ▼  by  1
```

Page 39

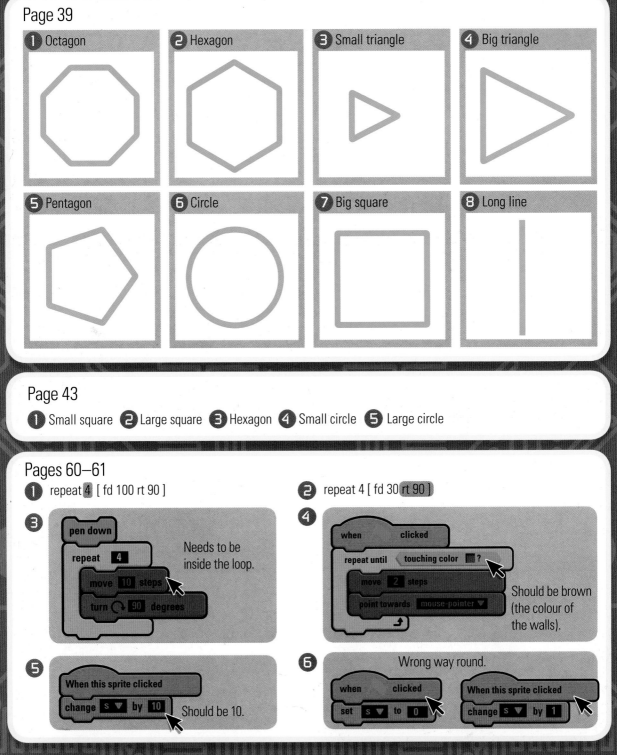

1 Octagon

2 Hexagon

3 Small triangle

4 Big triangle

5 Pentagon

6 Circle

7 Big square

8 Long line

Page 43

1 Small square **2** Large square **3** Hexagon **4** Small circle **5** Large circle

Pages 60–61

1 repeat **4** [fd 100 rt 90]

2 repeat 4 [fd 30 rt 90]

3

```
pen down
repeat    4
    move  10  steps
    turn  90  degrees
```

Needs to be inside the loop.

4

```
when         clicked
repeat until   touching color     ?
    move   2   steps
    point towards   mouse-pointer ▼
```

Should be brown (the colour of the walls).

5

```
When this sprite clicked
change  s ▼  by  10
```

Should be 10.

6 Wrong way round.

```
when        clicked
set  s ▼  to  0
```

```
When this sprite clicked
change  s ▼  by  1
```

Browser

www.qed-publishing.co.uk/extra-resources.php

CONTENTS :: CHAPTER 3

Enter ⏎

INTRODUCTION

Remember!

Remember!

This chapter will take your programming skills to the next level. We'll start off by working with the easy-to-use programming language Scratch. Then we will move on to a more complex language called Python. You are going to learn concepts including selection, how to use 'if' statements, and how to work with random numbers.

Refresh your memory

In chapter 2, we learnt how to work with Scratch and how to use loops and variables. In case you've forgotten, here's a quick refresher on all that.

Let's remind ourselves how Scratch works. You can make a sprite move around the 'stage' area in the top left of the screen. Commands are in the form of blocks, which you join together to make programs.

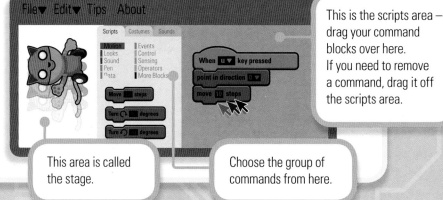

This is the scripts area – drag your command blocks over here. If you need to remove a command, drag it off the scripts area.

This area is called the stage.

Choose the group of commands from here.

Loops can be used to repeat commands. Both of these pieces of code draw a square.

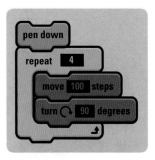

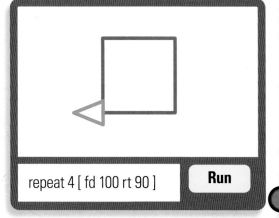

repeat 4 [fd 100 rt 90]   **Run**

Variables can be used to store information.

Age = 8

What you will learn

In the next few pages, you'll learn how to use 'if' statements to select different parts of a program.

```
When            clicked
ask  what animal am I?  and wait
  if  < answer  =  cat >  then
    say  Well done!
```

Quiz Master

Key word

Random: When all possible choices have an equal chance of being picked – they are not selected according to any pattern.

You'll learn how to write simple programs using a programming language called Python.

```
for n in range(1,101):
    print(n)
```

You will find out how to program with random numbers to make your own random pieces of art.

You'll even find out how to program a random sandwich using Python!

```
from random import *
f1=["cheese", "egg", "jam"]
f2=["carrot", "cress", "pickle"]
```

'IF' COMMANDS

I have made a plan of what we need to do.

Ask a question. If the answer is correct, say 'Well done'.

We need to use **if answer =**

Ask 'What animal am I?' If answer = cat, say 'Well done'.

Quiz Master

Sometimes we want to run different bits of code in response to a question or input in a program. We can do this by using 'if' commands. This is called selection. Let's make a quiz to try it out.

Question time

1

Start Scratch (see page 4) and click **'Create'** or **'Try it out'**. Click the **'Scripts'** tab in the centre of the Scratch screen. Select the **Events** group.

Drag a **'When green flag clicked'** code block to the scripts area.

Events
Control
Sensing

when ▲ clicked

Download our robots to use as sprites on Scratch! Go to http://www.qed-publishing.co.uk/extra-resources.php or scan here:

Key word

Selection: The way a computer program chooses which commands to run, after a simple question or value check.

What animal am I?

Click the green flag icon to test your code.

2

Click the **Sensing** group.

Drag an **'Ask and wait'** code block to join it.

Change the question text to 'What animal am I?'

Events
Control
Sensing
Operators
More Blocks

when ▲ clicked

ask What animal am I? and wait

?

cat ✓

3

Now we need our program to check if the answer is correct. Click the **Control** group.

Drag an **'If then'** code block to join your program.

- Events
- **Control**
- Sensing
- Operators
- More Blocks

when clicked
ask what animal am I? and wait
if ⬡ then

4

Click the **Operators** group.

Drag a green **'Equals'** box onto the **'If then'** block.

- Events
- Control
- Sensing
- **Operators**
- More Blocks

when clicked
ask What animal am I? and wait
if ■ = ■ then

The **=** operator is used to check if two values are the same.

■ = ■

5

Click the **Sensing** group.

Drag an **'Answer'** code block into the left square in the **'Equals'** block.

- Events
- Control
- **Sensing**
- Operators
- More Blocks

when clicked
ask what animal am I? and wait
if answer = ■ then

Now click inside the right-hand square in the **'Equals'** block and type in the correct answer: cat.

answer = cat

6

Click the **Looks** group.

Drag a **'Say Hello!'** code block into the middle of the **'If then'** block.

Change the text to say 'Well done!'.

Click the green flag icon to test your code.

- Motion
- **Looks**
- Sound
- Pen
- Data

ask what animal am I? and wa
if answer = cat
say Well done!

Challenge

Can you think of a more difficult question?

Saving your work

Click the **'File'** menu at the top of the page on the left. Then click:
Download to your computer – to save a file onto your computer.
Upload from your computer – to open a file you saved earlier.
New – to start some new work.

Quiz Mas...

QUIZ TIME

To make a better quiz, we need to find a way to ask several questions. We also need to keep a score of our right answers. To do this, we can add a score variable.

Capital quiz

1

Start Scratch.

Build a quiz with one question. Turn back to the previous page if you need help.

Change the question and answer text.

Test your code.

```
when          clicked
ask   What is the capital of England?   and wait
if   answer  =  London   then
    say   Well done!
```

2

We need to make the program wait before asking the next question.

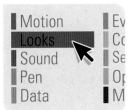

Click the **Looks** group.

Remove the **'Say Well Done!'** code block.

```
ask   What is the capital of England?   and wait
if   answer  =  London   then
    say   Well done!   for   2   secs
```

Replace it with a **'Say Hello! for 2 secs'** block. Change the text to 'Well done!'

3

Click the **Sensing** group.

Drag an **'Ask and wait'** code block to join after the **'If then'** block.

Type in the next question.

```
Control
Sensing          ask   What is the capital of France?   and w
Operators
```

4

Drag in code to check the answer to your second question. Turn back to the previous page if you need help.

Test your code.

```
if   answer  =  Paris   then
    say   Well done!   for   2   secs
```

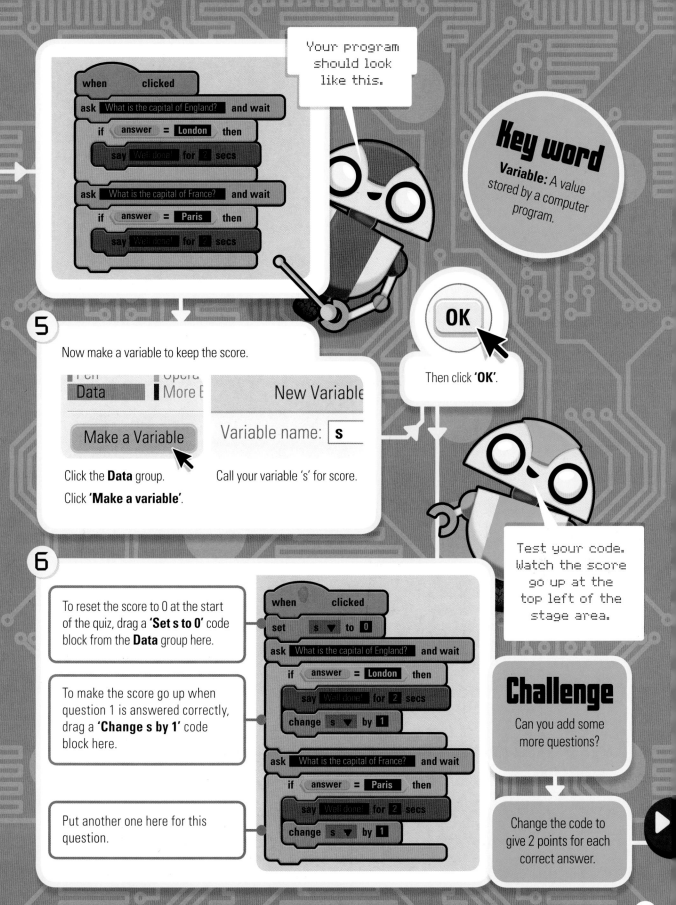

Your program should look like this.

```
when   clicked
ask  What is the capital of England?   and wait
  if   answer  =  London   then
    say  Well done!  for  2  secs

ask  What is the capital of France?   and wait
  if   answer  =  Paris   then
    say  Well done!  for  2  secs
```

Key word
Variable: A value stored by a computer program.

OK

Then click **'OK'**.

5

Now make a variable to keep the score.

```
Data        More E
Make a Variable
```

```
New Variable
Variable name:  S
```

Click the **Data** group.
Click **'Make a variable'**.

Call your variable 's' for score.

Test your code. Watch the score go up at the top left of the stage area.

6

To reset the score to 0 at the start of the quiz, drag a **'Set s to 0'** code block from the **Data** group here.

To make the score go up when question 1 is answered correctly, drag a **'Change s by 1'** code block here.

Put another one here for this question.

```
when   clicked
set   s ▼  to  0
ask  What is the capital of England?   and wait
  if   answer  =  London   then
    say  Well done!  for  2  secs
    change  s ▼  by  1

ask  What is the capital of France?   and wait
  if   answer  =  Paris   then
    say  Well done!  for  2  secs
    change  s ▼  by  1
```

Challenge

Can you add some more questions?

Change the code to give 2 points for each correct answer.

'ELSE' COMMANDS

Key word
Operator: A piece of code that carries out a mathematical or logical operation.

We've learnt how to use selection to check if something is true. What about if it is false – if someone gives the wrong answer to a question? We can use 'else' commands to run a different bit of code in this case.

Wrong answer

1

Start Scratch.

Make one question. Turn to page 68 for help if you need it.

Change the question text.

```
when        clicked
ask  What is 10 + 10?   and wait
```

2

Click the **Control** group.

Drag an **'If then else'** code block to join your program.

| Events |
| Control |
| Sensing |
| Operators |
| More Blocks |

```
ask  What is 10 + 10?   and wait
if           then

else

```

3

Drag in code to check the answer to the question.

If you need help, turn back to page 69.

```
ask  What is 10 + 10?   and wait
if      answer = 20      then
```

4

Now we need to make the program give a message to the player, depending on their answer.

| Motion |
| Looks |
| Sound |
| Pen |
| Data |

```
ask  What is 10 + 10?   and wait
if      answer = 20    then
    say  Correct  for 2 secs
else
    say  Wrong  for 2 secs
```

Drag a **'Say for 2 secs'** code block into the top gap and type in 'Correct'.

Drag a **'Say for 2 secs'** code block into the bottom gap and type in 'Wrong'.

Now try adding another question to your quiz. Use another **'If then else'** code block so the player gets told if each answer is right or wrong.

Higher or lower?

We know how to check if an answer, or variable, is equal to a value. Now we will learn to use 'Less than' or 'More than' operators to compare how big a variable is. We are going to make a small program that checks how old the player is before it starts.

1

Start a new program.

```
⊕ File ▾   Edit ▾
    New
```

Make code to ask 'How old are you?'

```
when      clicked
ask  How old are you?  and wait
```

2

From the **Control** group, drag an **'If then else'** code block to join your program.

```
ask  How old are you?  and wait
if            then

else
```

Click the **Operators** group.

Drag a **'Less than'** code block onto the **'If then else'** block.

```
Sensing        ask  How old are you?  and
Operators
More Blocks     if   ■ < ■   then
```

3

Click the **Sensing** group. Drag an **'Answer'** code block into the left square in the **'Less than'** block. Type '8' into the right square.

```
answer  <  8
```

4

Click the **Looks** group.

```
Motion      ask  How old are you?  and wait
Looks       if   answer < 8   then
Sound           say  You are too young!  for  2  secs
Pen
Data        else
                say  Enjoy the game.  for  2  secs
```

Drag a **'Say for 2 secs'** code block into the top gap and type in a message.

Drag a **'Say for 2 secs'** code block into the bottom gap and type in a message.

You can add a 'Stop' command after the 'Say' command to stop the program.

```
Stop  all ▾
```

Challenge

Try making the 'How old are you?' program using the 'More than' operator instead of 'Less than'.

You can start the rest of your program below here. Only players aged 8 and over could use it.

IF SPRITE IS TOUCHED...

Selection can be really useful in games. For example, we can use 'If then' command blocks to check if one sprite has touched another.

Apple-eating game

We are going to make a game where a cat sprite has to eat four apples. We will have to make lots of apple sprites by duplicating them.

We need to plan this in three parts.

1.
Move the cat to follow the mouse cursor.

2.
If the cat has touched an apple, hide the apple and make the score go up.

3.
Make lots of apples!

1

First we will drag code to the scripts area to make the Scratch sprite move slowly across the screen, pointing towards the mouse pointer.

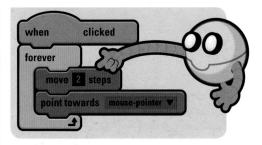

Drag the **'When green flag clicked'** code block from the **Events** group. Get the **'Forever'** loop block from the **Control** group, and the other blocks from the **Motion** group. Change the speed of the sprite to move 2 steps each loop.

Click the green flag icon near the top of the Scratch screen to test your code.

2

Click the **Data** group to make a variable called 's' for the score.

Look at step 5 on page 71 for help.

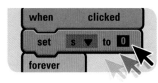

Drag a **'Set s to 0'** code block above the **'Forever'** loop.

3

Now add an apple sprite.

Click this icon.

Scroll down to the apple and click on it.

OK Then click **'OK'**.

I'm making an apple disappear!

74

4

Now we will drag code to the scripts area to control the apple.

Get the **'When green flag clicked'** code block from the **Events** group.

Get the **'Show'** code block from the **Looks** group and the **'Forever'** loop from the **Control** group.

The **'Show'** code block will make sure the apple is visible at the start of the game.

5

Every loop, we must check if the cat has touched the apple. If it has, the score must go up.

Join together these blocks of code.

You'll find the **'If then'** block in the **Control** group, the **'Touching'** block in the **Sensing** group, the **'Hide'** block in the **Looks** group, and the **'Change s by 1'** block in the **Data** group.

Set the **'Touching'** code block to 'Sprite1' – the cat.

6

If the apple is touching the cat, the apple will hide and the score will go up by 1.

Drag the **'If then'** code block into the **'Forever'** loop.

This will mean the **'If touching'** check will run on every loop forever.

7

Finally, right-click the apple and click **'Duplicate'**. (If you're using a Mac, you'll need to hold the **'Control'** key and click.)

Drag the new apple to a space and then duplicate two more apples.

Test your game!

When the apples are duplicated, their code is duplicated too!

Challenge

Make your own game with different sprites. How about making the apples move when the flag is clicked?

STARTING PYTHON

Python is a computer language that will help you learn more complex ideas and techniques. In Scratch, we dragged commands around to make a program. With Python, you need to type all the commands very carefully to make your programs work.

Installing Python

Python is free to download, and comes with something called IDLE which lets you type and edit Python programs.

You need to download and install Python before you start coding. Ask an adult to help you. Check that they don't mind you installing some software on the computer. See page 4 for help.

Using Python

1. Start IDLE, the Python editor.

ON A WINDOWS COMPUTER

Click **'Start'**
       'Programs'
       'Python'
       'IDLE'

On Windows 8, go to top right of the screen:

Click **'Search'**
Type **'idle'**
Click on the program to run it

ON A MAC

Click **'Spotlight'** 🔍 (top right of the screen)

Type **'idle'**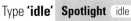

Press **'Enter'** ⏎

Woohoo... download!

2. Click **'File'** then **'New file'**.

3 The command **print** tells Python to display text on the screen. Type this code:

```
print ("hello")
```

Make sure you type commands in lower case, not capitals!

Your text will change colour automatically to show parts of the code. **Print** will be purple and **"hello"** will be green.

Make sure you type really carefully. You need both brackets and both quotes for your code to work.

4 You must save your code before you run it.

Click **'File'** then **'Save'** (to the desktop). Name as **'test'** then press **'Enter'**.

5 Run your code!

Click **'Run'** then **'Run module'**.

```
print ("hello")
```

```
>>>
hello
>>>
```

The output from your program will be shown in another window.

If it doesn't work, check your code carefully and try again.

Congratulations!
You have made your first Python program. Click **'File'** then **'Exit'** and practise steps 1 to 5 again.

Change your program to say something else, like...

'Goodbye!'

PYTHON PRINTING

Hello!

Now we are going to write a few simple Python programs. To start off, we are going to practise using Python to print text on the screen. Then we'll get Python to do simple calculations and print the answer.

Hello world!

1. Start IDLE, the Python editor. Turn back to page 76 for help if you need it.

2. Click **'File'** then **'New'**.

3. Type your code:
   print("hello")
   print("world")

   Press **'Enter'** after each line.

4. Click **'File'** then **'Save'**. Choose a file name and press **'Enter'**.

5. Click **'Run'**, then **'Run module'** to test your code. The output from your program should look like this:

   ```
   >>>
   hello
   world
   >>>
   ```

Making calculations

1. Click **'File'** then '**New**'.

2. Type your code:
   print("ten plus ten is")
   print(10 + 10)

   You don't need quotes when doing a calculation.

3. Save then run your code. (Look at steps 4 and 5 on the right.) The output should look like this:

   ```
   >>>
   ten plus ten is
   20
   >>>
   ```

This is how Python runs a program with several lines of code.

78

Do your sums

Now try typing in the following programs. Follow the usual steps to start a new program, save it and run it each time.

1
```
print("twenty plus twenty is")
print(20 + 20)
```

2
```
print("fifty plus twenty is")
print(50 + 20)
```

3
```
print("ten times ten is")
print(10 * 10)
```

4
```
print("four plus four is")
print(4 + 4)
print("eight times eight is")
print(8 * 8)
```

See page 92 for the answers.

Computer programs use **✱** instead of **x** to do multiplication.

Remember: you don't need quotes when doing calculations, but you do need brackets!

Shortcuts

A quick way to save your work is to hold down **'Control'** and press **S**. (On a Mac, hold ⌘ then press **S**.)

A shortcut to running your code is just pressing the **F5** key at the top of the keyboard.

Challenge

Write a program with your own sums and calculations in.

Use **-** to do subtraction and **/** to do division.

Can you make a program to work out the number of hours in a year?

PYTHON QUESTIONS

After working with Scratch, using Python can seem a bit more fiddly. However, there are some things that can be done very easily with Python. We're going to use inputs, variables and 'if' commands to code a simple quiz.

Is that you?

1. Start IDLE, the Python editor. Turn back to page 76 for help if you need it.

2. Click **'File'** then **'New'**.

3. We need to make Python ask a question. Type in this code:

```
name=input("what is your name? ")
```

4. Click **'File'** then **'Save'**. Choose a file name and press **'Enter'**.

5. Click **'Run'** then **'Run module'** to test your code. The output from your program should look like this:

```
>>>
what is your name? ←
>>>
```

> Type your answer here and press **'Enter'**.

6. We want Python to say 'hello' to the user. Add a second line to your code:

```
name=input("what is your name?")
print("hello", name)
```

Save and run your code. What do you think will happen?

> What is your name?

> Errr...

> The first line of code tells Python to store what the user types in a variable called 'name'.

> The second line tells it to print 'hello' and whatever it stored.

7 We can change our code so it only says 'hello' if your name is Max.

```
name=input("what is your name?")
if name=="Max":
--->    print("Hello coder!")
```

Type in this code.

IDLE should put in a tab here for you. If not, press the **'Tab'** key yourself!

8 Save and run your code to test it. Try changing the name you type.

...errr...

Max?!?

Key word

Input: An action (like typing in an answer) that tells a program to do something.

Make sure you type everything very carefully:

Two equals signs

Colon

:

```
if name=="Max":
--->    print("Hello coder!")
```

Tab

The 'if' command checks if something is true. The next line only runs if it is true.

Hello coder!

Quiz time

Now you know enough to code your own quiz. Start with the question shown here: 'What is the capital of England?' Then, try adding some more questions of your own.

```
a=input("what is the capital of England?")
if a=="London":
    print("Correct")
```

```
>>>
what is the capital of England? London
Correct
>>>
```

PYTHON LOOPS

We've already looked at how we can print things on the screen with Python. Now we are going to learn how to use loops in Python that will allow us to print things over and over again.

Why use loops?

1. Start up Python (see page 76).
2. Type in the following program:

```
print(1)
print(2)
print(3)
print(4)
print(5)
```

3. Save and run the program. You should see the numbers 1 to 5 printed on the screen.

```
>>>
1
2
3
4
5
>>>
```

If we wanted to count up to 10, we could add more print commands. But if we wanted to count up to 100, it would take a very long time to program. It would also mean we had to change the program every time we wanted to count to a different number.

Instead we can create a loop to count up to any number very easily. We need to use the 'for' command:

Variable (called **n**) to do the counting. You could call it any letter you like.

Starting number

Number above the highest number we want to count to

Don't forget the colon.

```
for n in range(1,11):
    print(n)
```

IDLE should put in a tab here for you. If not, press the **'Tab'** key yourself!

Put any commands you want to be repeated here. In this case, it's the commands to print out the numbers 1–10.

Key word

Loop: A series of commands repeated a number of times.

Counting to 100

1 Start up Python and type in the following program:

```
for n in range(1,101):
    print(n)
```

2 Save and run the program.

You should see the numbers 1 to 100 whizz by on the screen.

```
>>>
1
2
…
98
99
100
>>>
```

print ("DANGER!")
print ("DANGER!")

print ("number stampede!")

Have a go

Type in these programs. Before you run them, try to predict what they will do. Check your answers on page 92.

1
```
for n in range(1,21):
    print(n)
```

2
```
for n in range(1,51):
    print(n)
```

3
```
for a in range(1,201):
    print(a)
```

4
```
for b in range(1,101):
    print(b*10)
```

5
```
for c in range(1,101):
    print(c*100)
```

Remember
* means
multiply.

83

PYTHON GRAPHICS

We can draw graphics – such as diagrams and pictures – in Python by borrowing a special group of commands called a library. We need to tell Python we are going to use the library at the start of our program. We can then use commands in a similar way to how we directed the turtle or sprite in Logo and Scratch (Chapter 1).

Turtle time

A turtle is a robot, sprite or arrow that can be given commands to move around. In Python, the library of commands that allows us to draw pictures is called the 'turtle library'. It tells the turtle – an arrow – how to move and draw. We are going to learn how to use it.

1 Start up Python.

2 Type in the following program:

```
from turtle import *
forward(200)
```

This tells Python to borrow all the commands from the turtle library and bring them into our program.

3 Save and run the program. A new window will open to show the turtle graphics. The **forward(200)** command will draw a line like this:

4 We can make the turtle turn left and right by using commands called **left** and **right**! Try adding these commands to your program:

```
from turtle import *
forward(200)
right(90)
forward(200)
right(90)
```

This tells the turtle to make a right turn of 90 degrees – a right angle.

Make sure there isn't a space at the start of a line.

Save and run the program.

Now try this

Try these exercises. Check your answers on page 92!

1 Add more code to finish drawing a square.

2 Try changing your code to draw a rectangle.

Don't forget to type **from turtle import *** at the start of your program.

Loops and graphics

On page 82, we found out how loops can repeat commands when counting. We can use the same idea to draw shapes. We will use a variable called **n** to count the number of times to repeat the loop. Type in this code:

```
from turtle import *
for n in range(0,4):
    forward(200)
    right(90)
```

This loop draws four sides of a square. We could pick any letter as a counting variable. We have used **n**.

The colon will add a tab to the start of the next line.

On page 82,

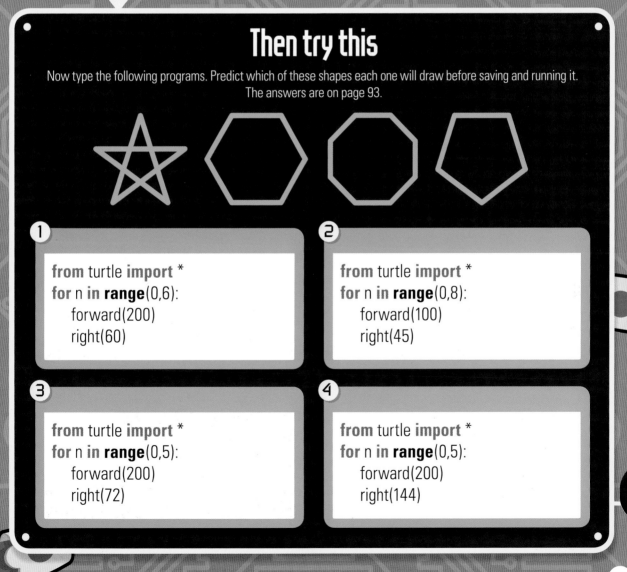

Then try this

Now type the following programs. Predict which of these shapes each one will draw before saving and running it. The answers are on page 93.

1
```
from turtle import *
for n in range(0,6):
    forward(200)
    right(60)
```

2
```
from turtle import *
for n in range(0,8):
    forward(100)
    right(45)
```

3
```
from turtle import *
for n in range(0,5):
    forward(200)
    right(72)
```

4
```
from turtle import *
for n in range(0,5):
    forward(200)
    right(144)
```

The answers are on page 93.

Key word

Library: A collection of commands that are already stored and ready for use.

RANDOM PYTHON

It would be dull if games were always the same each time we played them. With a board game, we can throw a dice to choose how far a player moves each time. In a computer game, we can get the computer to pick a random number.

randint(1,6)

Randint means 'random integer' (a random whole number).

Between 1 and 6

Random number

1. Start up Python and type in the below command. **Random** tells Python that we are going to use random numbers. **Import** tells Python to borrow commands from a library to do this.

```
from random import *
```

2. Now print a random number:

```
from random import *
print(randint(1,6))
```

3. Save and run the program. A number between 1 and 6 will be shown. Each time you run the program, a new number will be picked. For example:

```
>>>
3
>>>
```

```
>>>
5
>>>
```

```
>>>
2
>>>
```

Heads or tails?

We can also mimic tossing a coin. We are going to use a command called **choice**, which will pick a word from a list.

1. Start a new Python program. Type in:

```
from random import *
coin=["heads", "tails"]
print(choice(coin))
```

This makes a list of two words called 'coin'. Make sure you type the double quotes and square brackets carefully.

This tells Python to pick a word randomly from the list called 'coin'.

2. Save and run the program. The program will print 'heads' or 'tails'. Run the program again to test it.

```
>>>
heads
>>>
```

```
>>>
tails
>>>
```

```
>>>
tails
>>>
```

86

Make a sandwich

Finally we are going to teach Python how to make a sandwich. We are going to make two lists of fillings and randomly pick one from each.

1 Click **'File'** and **'New file'** to start a new Python program.

2 Type in:

```
from random import *
f1=["cheese", "egg", "jam"]
f2=["carrot", "cress", "pickle"]
```

3 Add a final line:

```
print(choice(f1), "and", choice(f2))
```

4 Save and run the program to see a random sandwich!

```
>>>
jam and pickle
>>>
```

```
>>>
cheese and cress
>>>
```

5 Now you could change your code to make 10 sandwiches at once, using a 'for' loop:

```
from random import *
f1=["cheese", "egg", "jam"]
f2=["carrot", "cress", "pickle"]
for s in range(0,10):
    print(choice(f1),"and", choice(f2), "sandwich")
```

Key word

Import: To take data from one program into another.

Here is a list of my favourite fillings. Don't forget the commas and double quotes. Add a square bracket at each end.

My list is called f2.

Challenge

Add a third filling by making another list called f3.

RANDOM ART

Let's turn back to Scratch to see how we can use random numbers to control computer graphics. By picking random numbers for the place we draw a circle, how big and what colour it is, we can make a random piece of art.

Coordinates

We choose where to draw by setting the x and y coordinates of the sprite:

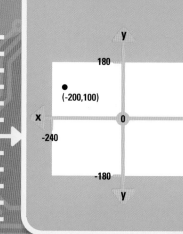

'Set x to' tells Scratch how far to place the sprite to the left or right of the screen.

'Set y to' tells Scratch how far to place the sprite up or down the screen.

Random bubble art

1 Start Scratch. See page 4 for help. Click the **Pen** group. Drag a **'Clear'** and a **'Pen down'** code block to the scripts area.

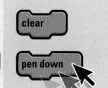

2 Click the **Control** group. Drag a **'Repeat'** code block beneath them. Change it to make 20 loops.

3 Click the **Motion** group. Drag a **'Set x to'** and a **'Set y to'** code block into the **'Repeat'** loop.

4 To make the lines random, click the **Operators** group. Drag a **'Pick random'** code block into the circle of the **'Set x to'** code block. Do the same for the **'Set y to'** block.

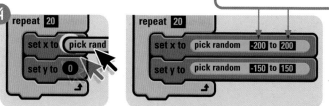

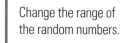

Change the range of the random numbers.

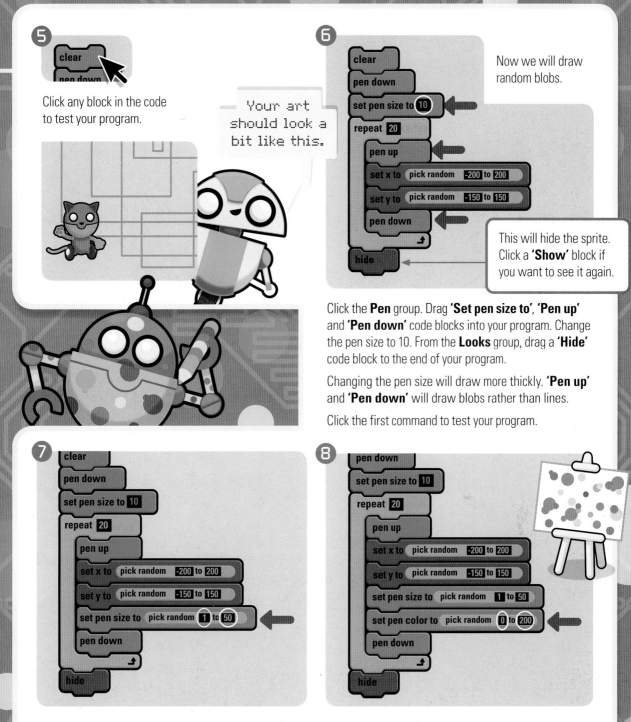

5

`clear`
`pen down`

Click any block in the code to test your program.

Your art should look a bit like this.

6

`clear`
`pen down`
`set pen size to 10`
`repeat 20`
  `pen up`
  `set x to pick random -200 to 200`
  `set y to pick random -150 to 150`
  `pen down`
`hide`

Now we will draw random blobs.

This will hide the sprite. Click a **'Show'** block if you want to see it again.

Click the **Pen** group. Drag **'Set pen size to'**, **'Pen up'** and **'Pen down'** code blocks into your program. Change the pen size to 10. From the **Looks** group, drag a **'Hide'** code block to the end of your program.

Changing the pen size will draw more thickly. **'Pen up'** and **'Pen down'** will draw blobs rather than lines.

Click the first command to test your program.

7

`clear`
`pen down`
`set pen size to 10`
`repeat 20`
  `pen up`
  `set x to pick random -200 to 200`
  `set y to pick random -150 to 150`
  `set pen size to pick random 1 to 50`
  `pen down`
`hide`

You can change the size of the blobs by adding another **'Set pen size'** and a **'Pick random'** code block (from the **Operators** group). Change the range of random numbers to choose the smallest and biggest blob size. Test it!

8

`pen down`
`set pen size to 10`
`repeat 20`
  `pen up`
  `set x to pick random -200 to 200`
  `set y to pick random -150 to 150`
  `set pen size to pick random 1 to 50`
  `set pen color to pick random 0 to 200`
  `pen down`
`hide`

Finally add a **'Set pen color to 0'** (note the American spelling of 'color') from the **Pen** group and a **'Pick random'** code block (from the **Operators** group) in to your program. Choose the range of colours you want. Test your program. Now experiment with all the random number ranges and how many times the loop runs.

DEBUGGING

Coding can be a process of trial and error – testing ideas and seeing if they work. It is normal to make mistakes when coding. A bug is another name for a mistake in a piece of code that stops it working properly. Debugging means fixing those mistakes. Try these exercises then check your answers on page 93.

1

This Scratch program should only say 'Well done' when the answer is 4. But it says 'Well done' all the time. Debug it!

```
when  clicked
ask  What is 2 x 2?  and wait
if   answer  =  4   then

say  Well done
```

2

This program should only say 'Well done' when the answer is 25. But it says 'Well done' except when the answer is 25. What's gone wrong?

```
when  clicked
ask  What is 5 x 5?  and wait
if   answer  =  25   then
    say  Wrong
else
    say  Well done
```

3

This code is part of a game where a dog has to catch a cat. The player should get one point when it does – but the score goes back to 0 instead. Fix the code.

```
Score  0

when  clicked
change  score ▼  by  1
forever
    if   touching  Cat1 ▼  ?   then
        set  score ▼  to  0
```

Python debugging

4

There are some small errors in each of these lines of Python code, so nothing is being shown. Debug each line.

a

```
prinnt("Hello everyone!")
```

b

```
Print("This is my program.")
```

c

```
print("Goodbye - hope you enjoyed it!)
```

5

This code should print the numbers from 1 to 10, but it stops at 9. Debug it!

```
for n in range(1,10):
    print(n)
```

6

Nothing happens with this code. It should print the numbers from 1 to 20. What's wrong?

```
for n in range(1,21):
print(n)
```

7

This code should print a random number between 1 and 6, but instead it always prints a 6. Debug it!

```
from random import *
print(randint(6,6))
```

Debugging guidelines

When your code doesn't do what you want it to:

1. Work through your code step by step, thinking about what each command does.
2. Draw a picture or diagram to help.
3. Have a break for a few minutes!

Think about these guidelines when you are coding:

1. Plan your program carefully – either with a diagram or some notes.
2. When you are learning to code, it is better to write lots of small, simple programs rather than one larger and more complex program.
3. Test your program as you build it. Don't wait until you have put in all the commands.

CHAPTER 3 ANSWERS

Page 79

1
```
>>>
twenty plus twenty is
40
>>>
```

2
```
>>>
fifty plus twenty is
70
>>>
```

3
```
>>>
ten times ten is
100
>>>
```

4
```
>>>
four plus four is
8
eight times eight is
64
>>>
```

Page 84

1 **from** turtle **import** *
```
forward(200)
right(90)
forward(200)
right(90)
forward(200)
right(90)
forward(200)
right(90)
```

2 **from** turtle **import** *
```
forward(200)
right(90)
forward(100)
right(90)
forward(200)
right(90)
forward(100)
right(90)
```

Page 83

1 1 2 3... 19 20

2 1 2 3... 49 50

3 1 2 3... 199 200

4 10 20 30... 990 1000

5 100 200 300... 9900 10000

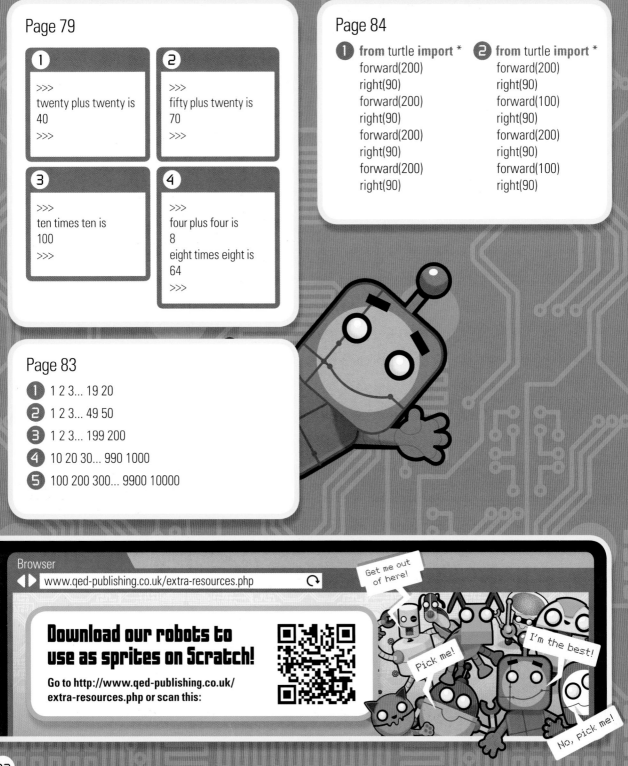

Browser

www.qed-publishing.co.uk/extra-resources.php

Download our robots to use as sprites on Scratch!

Go to http://www.qed-publishing.co.uk/extra-resources.php or scan this:

Get me out of here!

Pick me!

I'm the best!

No, pick me!

Page 85

1 Hexagon

2 Octagon

3 Pentagon

4 Star

Page 90–91

1
```
when  clicked
ask  What is 2 x 2?  and wait
if  answer = 4  then

say  Well done
```
Needs to be inside the loop

2
```
when  clicked
ask  What is 5 x 5?  and wait
if  answer = 25  then
  say  Wrong
else
  say  Well done
```
Wrong way round

3
```
when  clicked
change  score  by  1
forever
  if  touching  Cat1 ?  then
    set  score  to  0
```
Wrong way round

4 a) **prinnt** should be **print** (only 1 n)
b) **Print** should be **print** (not capital P)
c) **it!)** should be **it!")** (missing quote at end)

5 **range(1,11)** not **(1,10)**

6 **print(n)** should start with a tab:
   ......**print(n)**

7 **randint(1,6)** not **(6,6)**

93

CONTENTS :: CHAPTER 4

Enter

INTRODUCTION

You probably use the World Wide Web every day to find out information, check out the news or watch music videos. In this chapter, you will find out how web pages are built and learn to create your own web pages using HTML and JavaScript.

What is the web?

Computers can be connected together by cables and, often today, by wireless links. Computers that are connected together are called a **network**. A network can be used to share information and resources.

The internet is a global network of computers. It is used for things like the web, email and downloading music.

The World Wide Web (or web for short) uses the internet to share web pages.

Key word

Internet: An enormous network of computers connected across the whole world.

Did you know?

The web was invented by the British computer scientist Tim Berners-Lee in 1989.

Getting around the web

All pages on the web have their own special address so that we can go straight to them when we need them — rather like a postal address takes us straight to the right house on the right street. The address is called a **URL**, which stands for Uniform Resource Locator. Pages are often linked together with **hyperlinks**. Clicking on these links takes us from one page to another.

What is HTTP?

All things that use the internet have to obey their own set of rules for how to share information. If they didn't, everyone would be doing things in a different way and we wouldn't all be able to share information across the world. These rules are called **protocols**. The protocol used for the World Wide Web is called the Hypertext Transfer Protocol (HTTP). You have probably seen the letters 'http' at the start of web addresses. HTTP is the standard way to transport web pages over the internet.

What is HTML?

Web pages are written in a special language or code called HTML (Hypertext Mark-up Language). This chapter will teach you how to use HTML to make your own pages.

```
Text editor – headings.html

<html>
  <h1>London</h1>
  <p>England</p>
  <h1>Paris</h1>
  <p>France</p>
</html>
```

JavaScript

This chapter will also teach you how to add JavaScript to your web pages. JavaScript is a programming language that you can use within a web page to make it more interactive.

```
<script>
  for(var n=1; n<10; n++)
    document.write(n);
</script>
```

Key word

World Wide Web:
A system that uses the internet to connect pages of information from around the world.

What is a server?

To share the web pages you create over the internet, you would need to load them onto a special computer called a server. But don't worry: to learn to create web pages, you just need to work on a normal desktop computer or laptop. You can keep your web pages private for now!

What is a browser?

In order to look at a web page, we need to use a special program called a browser. Popular browsers include Chrome, Firefox, Internet Explorer and Safari. A browser uses HTTP to access web pages and then interprets the code in the HTML to display the web pages on our computer screen.

CREATING WEB PAGES

If you want to make a page of information that can be shown online, you need to write it using a code, or language, called HTML. We need to use a program called a text editor to write our HTML and a browser to view it in.

HTML uses tags

To show what goes on a web page we use special codes called tags.

Tags always have angle brackets < > around them.

The page must start with an **opening HTML** tag.

Text editor – mypage.html

```
<html>
        My web page
</html>
```

Everything between the tags is HTML.

The closing tag has a slash: **/**

It ends with a **closing HTML** tag.

Now get started!

To get started, we are going to make some simple web pages. You can store them on your computer instead of on the internet. This will make it quicker and safer to test and try out ideas.

You will need a text editor and a web browser to do this. See page 123 for help on finding them. You will probably already have a **web browser** on your computer. This is the program you use to view pages on the web.

A text editor is a special kind of word processor, a bit like the program you use to type a story or a letter. You probably already have one on your computer: **Notepad** on a PC, and **TextEdit** on a Mac.

Key word

Tags: Special words used to describe what objects there are on a web page.

Create a web page on your computer

1

ON A **WINDOWS** COMPUTER

Click: **'Start'**, **'Programs'**, **'Accessories'**, **'Notepad'**

For Windows 8: At top right of the screen, click **'Search'**, type **'Notepad'**, then click the program.

ON A **MAC**

Click **'Spotlight'** 🔍 (top right of the screen)

Type **textedit**

Spotlight   textedit

Press **'Enter'**

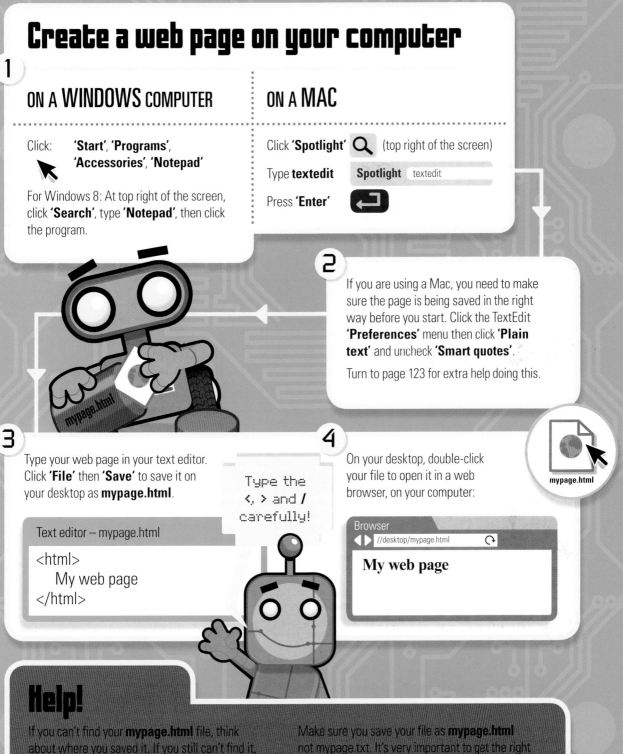

2

If you are using a Mac, you need to make sure the page is being saved in the right way before you start. Click the TextEdit **'Preferences'** menu then click **'Plain text'** and uncheck **'Smart quotes'**.

Turn to page 123 for extra help doing this.

3

Type your web page in your text editor. Click **'File'** then **'Save'** to save it on your desktop as **mypage.html**.

Type the <, > and / carefully!

Text editor – mypage.html

```
<html>
    My web page
</html>
```

4

On your desktop, double-click your file to open it in a web browser, on your computer:

mypage.html

Browser
//desktop/mypage.html

My web page

Help!

If you can't find your **mypage.html** file, think about where you saved it. If you still can't find it, start again from step 1 and try saving your file on the desktop. Then move the text editor to one side (by dragging the title) so you can see the file on the desktop.

Make sure you save your file as **mypage.html** not mypage.txt. It's very important to get the right extension (html not txt). If you get the wrong extension or no extension at all, check that 'Hide extension' and 'If no extension provided, use txt' are not ticked when you save.

USING HTML

We are going to have a look in more detail at an HTML page. Each object on the page has a special tag to tell the page what it is. We are going to learn about how to use different tags.

Making headings

1

Open up your text editor. For instructions, turn back to page 99.

2

In your text editor, type:

h1 means heading.

Text editor

```
<html>
    <h1>My story</h1>
    <p>Once upon a time</p>
</html>
```

P means paragraph.

3

Save your file as **headings.html**.

4

headings.html

Find your file and double-click it.

5

You should now see your page looking like this:

Browser

◀▶ //desktop/headings.html ↻

My story

Once upon a time

Arrange your desktop so you have your text editor on the left of the screen and your web browser on the right. This will make it easier for you to experiment and see the effects.

Text editor – headings.html

```
<html>
    <h1>My short story</h1>
    <p>Once upon a time</p>
</html>
```

Browser

◀▶ //desktop/headings.html ↻

My short story

Once upon a time

Try changing a few words. Then click **'File'** and **'Save'**.

Press the **'Refresh'** button to see changes.

Other tags

There are lots of tags you can use within normal text to emphasize certain words or to create different types of headings. Try adding some of these tags into your page. Remember to put opening tags before the words you want to change. Spend some time making small changes, saving and refreshing your page each time.

Tag	Description	Example	Appearance
<h1>	Main heading	<h1>Europe</h1>	**Europe**
<h3>	Minor heading	<h3>United Kingdom</h3>	**United Kingdom**
<strong>	Strong text (bold)	It was <strong>very</strong> tasty.	It was **very** tasty.
<em>	Emphasized text (italic)	It was <em>very</em> tasty.	It was *very* tasty.
<mark>	Highlighted text	10 20 <mark>30</mark> 40 50 60	10 20 30 40 50 60

Now try these

Try typing in the HTML below. Save and refresh to see how each page looks.
Then check the answers on page 122.

① Text editor – headings.html

```
<html>
      <h1>Cyber Cafe</h1>
      <p>Open every day</p>
</html>
```

② Text editor – headings.html

```
<html>
      <h1>Code School</h1>
      <h2>Smith Street</h2>
      <p>Learn to code</p>
</html>
```

③ Text editor – headings.html

```
<html>
      <h1>Huge</h1>
      <h3>Medium</h3>
      <h5>Tiny</h5>
</html>
```

④ Text editor – headings.html

```
<html>
      <h1>London</h1>
      <p>England</p>
      <h1>Paris</h1>
      <p>France</p>
</html>
```

It doesn't matter how you line up or 'indent' your HTML code. In this chapter, we show our HTML code with indents to make it easier to read. Most coders do this when writing web pages.

Make sure your file name ends in **.html** or it won't work!

ADDRESSES AND LINKS

Deliver WHERE?!?

Every page on the web has its own address. Most pages also have hyperlinks. Clicking one of these links takes you to another page or another website. We are going to find out how addresses and hyperlinks work.

Understanding web addresses

Just as every house has its own address, each page on the web has its own special address – a URL.

URL means Uniform Resource Locator.

Browser

www.mysite.co.uk/mypage.html

My web page

Each part of the address tells us something about the page and where it is:

www.mysite.co.uk/mypage.html

| Most web pages start with www. | The website is probably based in the United Kingdom. | The page is called mypage. | The page type is HTML. |

Web addresses around the world

The part of the URL before the slash **/** is called the domain. The last part of the domain tells us where the page is from. For example:

.uk means the UK	**.au** means Australia
.za means South Africa	**.de** means Germany
.es means Spain	**.ca** means Canada

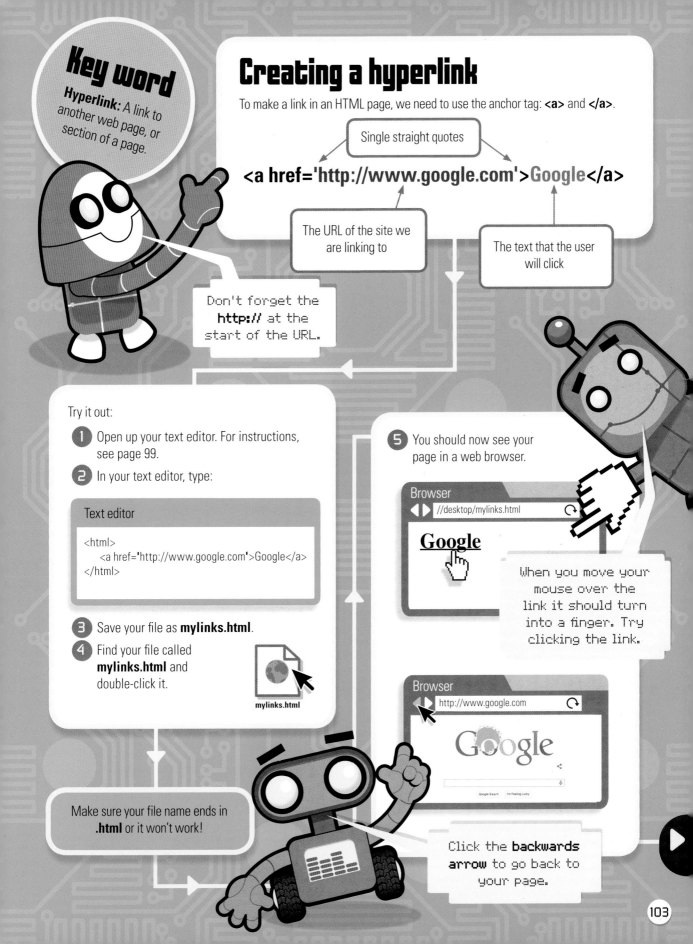

Key word

Hyperlink: A link to another web page, or section of a page.

Creating a hyperlink

To make a link in an HTML page, we need to use the anchor tag: **<a>** and **</a>**.

Single straight quotes

<a href='http://www.google.com'>Google</a>

The URL of the site we are linking to

The text that the user will click

Don't forget the **http://** at the start of the URL.

Try it out:

1 Open up your text editor. For instructions, see page 99.

2 In your text editor, type:

Text editor

```
<html>
    <a href='http://www.google.com'>Google</a>
</html>
```

3 Save your file as **mylinks.html**.

4 Find your file called **mylinks.html** and double-click it.

mylinks.html

Make sure your file name ends in **.html** or it won't work!

5 You should now see your page in a web browser.

Browser

//desktop/mylinks.html

Google

When you move your mouse over the link it should turn into a finger. Try clicking the link.

Browser

http://www.google.com

Google

Google Search   I'm Feeling Lucky

Click the **backwards arrow** to go back to your page.

LOTS OF LINKS

What sites will you choose?

Now we know how hyperlinks work, we are going to build a page that has links to a number of different websites. We will use heading and paragraph tags to add other text to our page.

My favourite sites

1

Open your text editor. If you've forgotten how, turn to page 99.

2

In your text editor, type:

Text editor

```
<html>
    <h1>My Favourite Sites</h1>
    <p>Click one of these:</p>
</html>
```

3

Save your file as **mypages.html** then double-click it to test it so far.

mypages.html

4

Arrange your desktop so you have your text editor on the left of the screen and your web browser on the right.

Press **'Refresh'** to see the changes.

Text editor – mypages.html

```
<html>
    <h1>My Favourite Sites</h1>
    <p>Click one of these:</p>
</html>
```

Browser

//desktop/mypages.html

My Favourite Sites

Click one of these:

Click **'File'** then **'Save'** after any changes.

5

Add a new anchor tag with a favourite website to your HTML page.

Save and refresh your page to test it.

Text editor – mypages.html

```
<html>
    <h1>My Favourite Sites</h1>
    <p>Click one of these:</p>
    <a href='http://www.google.com'>Google</a>
</html>
```

mypages.html

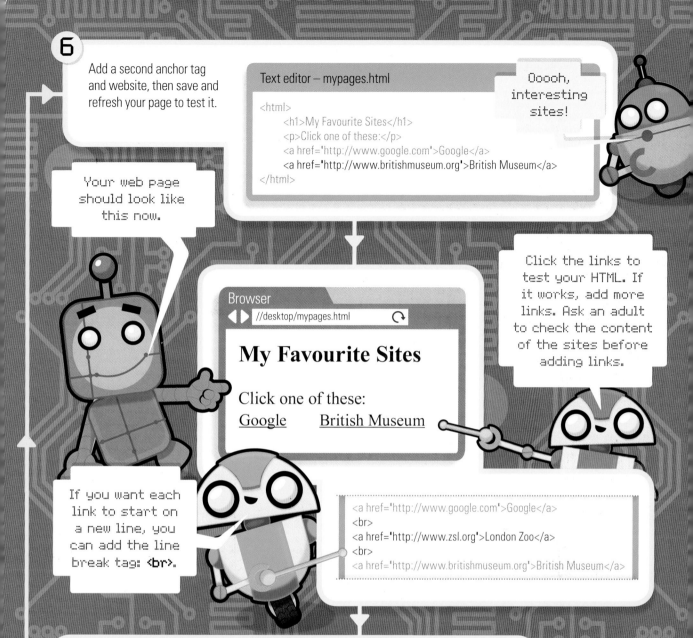

6 Add a second anchor tag and website, then save and refresh your page to test it.

Text editor – mypages.html

```
<html>
    <h1>My Favourite Sites</h1>
    <p>Click one of these:</p>
    <a href='http://www.google.com'>Google</a>
    <a href='http://www.britishmuseum.org'>British Museum</a>
</html>
```

Ooooh, interesting sites!

Your web page should look like this now.

Browser

//desktop/mypages.html

My Favourite Sites

Click one of these:
Google   British Museum

Click the links to test your HTML. If it works, add more links. Ask an adult to check the content of the sites before adding links.

If you want each link to start on a new line, you can add the line break tag: **
**.

```
<a href='http://www.google.com'>Google</a>
<br>
<a href='http://www.zsl.org'>London Zoo</a>
<br>
<a href='http://www.britishmuseum.org'>British Museum</a>
```

Using a more advanced text editor

You can keep using Notepad or TextEdit to make HTML pages for now. (If you're using a Mac, you may have problems with quote marks. Make sure you disable 'smart quotes' if you do use TextEdit to make bigger HTML pages – turn to page 123 for help.)

There are lots of programs that can help you make web pages, but to learn HTML and the other web technologies, you need a text editor that lets you stay in control of the code you type.

A text editor that is designed to help you code in HTML will do extra things to help you. It will change the colour of different parts of your code so it is easier to check. It will also make sure you have all the tags typed properly.

Sublime Text is a useful text editor that you can download and try out for free. Have a look at: **www.sublimetext.com**. See page 123 for more information about downloading it.

COLOUR IT!

We have found out how to add text and links onto a web page. Now we're going to learn how to change the colour of them. We will also meet the **<body>** tag, which holds all the things on the page together.

Coloured text

1 Start a new web page in your text editor. Type in:

Text editor
```
<html>
    <h1>Web</h1>
    <p>Tim Berners-Lee</p>
</html>
```

2 Save your file as **colour.html** then double-click it to test it so far.

colour.html

3 Arrange your desktop so you have your text editor on the left of the screen and your web browser on the right.

> Press the **'Refresh'** button to see any changes.

> Click **'File'** then **'Save'** after any changes.

Text editor – colour.html
```
<html>
    <h1>Web</h1>
    <p>Tim Berners-Lee</p>
```

Browser
//desktop/colour.html

Web

Tim Berners-Lee

4 Edit the second line so it looks like this:

Text editor – colour.html
```
<html>
    <h1 style='color:red'>Web</h1>
    <p>Tim Berners-Lee</p>
</html>
```

Do spell 'color' like this! It's the American spelling. Now save and refresh your page:

Browser
//desktop/colour.html

Web

Tim Berners-Lee

> Experiment by typing orange, blue and other colours instead of red.

5 Edit the third line so it looks like this. What happens?

Text editor – colour.html
```
<html>
    <h1 style='color:red'>Web</h1>
    <p style='color:green'>Tim Berners-Lee</p>
</html>
```

Changing the background colour

To change the colour of the page, first we need to add a **<body>** tag to our HTML.

It's a masterpiece!

The start of the body of the page

The end of the body of the page

Text editor – colour.html

```
<html>
  <body>
    <h1 style='color:red'>Web</h1>
    <p style='color:green'>Tim Berners-Lee</p>
  </body>
</html>
```

Now we can add the style 'attribute' to set the background colour:

Text editor – colour.html

```
<html>
  <body style='background-color:yellow'>
    <h1 style='color:red'>Web</h1>
    <p style='color:green'>Tim Berners-Lee</p>
  </body>
</html>
```

Save and refresh. The page should look like this:

Browser

//desktop/colour.html

Web

Tim Berners-Lee

Have a go

Now try typing in the HTML below. Check the answers on page 122.

1 Text editor – styles.html

```
<html>
  <h1 style='color:blue'>Tim Berners-Lee</h1>
  <p style='color:orange'>Ada Lovelace</p>
  <p style='color:green'>Alan Turing</p>
</html>
```

Save and refresh to see how each page looks.

2 Text editor – styles.html

```
<html>
  <body style='background-color:black'>
    <p style='color:yellow'>Nelson Mandela</p>
    <p style='color:green'>Mahatma Gandhi</p>
    <p style='color:white'>Rosa Parks</p>
  </body>
</html>
```

ADDING JAVASCRIPT

We've learnt how to use basic HTML to choose what goes on a web page. Now we will look at how to add code in a different language: JavaScript. JavaScript decides what the page actually does when we do things like click buttons. It can be used alongside HTML.

Click me

1

Start a new web page in your text editor. Type in this HTML:

Text editor

```
<html>
    <button>Click me</button>
</html>
```

2

Save your file as **hello.html** then double-click it to test it so far.

hello.html

Browser
//desktop/hello.html

> Click me

Try clicking the button... Why does nothing happen? We need to tell the button what to do when we click it! To do this we add a 'listener'. A listener will run JavaScript code when a particular event happens. We are going to use an onclick listener.

3

Now add some JavaScript to your code:

Single quotes around the JavaScript code

Text editor – hello.html

```
<html>
    <button onclick='alert("Hello")'>Click me</button>
</html>
```

Double quotes

If you have smart 'sloping' quotes, your code may not work. See page 123.

4

Save and refresh your file to test it.

Browser
//desktop/hello.html

> Click me

Hello

ALERT!

What does 'alert' mean?!?

Don't panic! **alert** is a JavaScript code word that tells the browser to show a message.

Key word

Listener: A line of code that is only run when a particular event happens, such as a button being clicked.

Greetings

1

Start a new web page in your text editor. Type in this HTML:

```
Text editor

<html>
  <button>Hello</button>
  <button>Goodbye</button>
</html>
```

2

Save your file as **greetings.html** then double-click it to test it. You should see something like this:

```
Browser

◀▶   //desktop/greetings.html        ↻

   Hello        Goodbye
```

The buttons are on the page but still need code to make them work.

This time we need to add two onclick listeners — one for each button.

3

Type in the following code, remembering to use single quotes and double quotes carefully — single quotes around the JavaScript, double quotes around the message.

```
Text editor – greetings.html

<html>
  <button onclick='alert("Hello")'>Hello</button>
  <button onclick='alert("Goodbye")'>Goodbye</button>
</html>
```

Challenge

Experiment with changing what is on the buttons and the messages that are displayed. Can you add a third button? What will it show when you click it?

4

Save and refresh your file to test it.

JAVASCRIPT LOOPS

If you have coded in languages like Scratch or Python, you will have come across loops and variables. Loops are sequences of commands that we want the computer to repeat. Variables are values that are stored by a computer. We will look at how to use these techniques in JavaScript.

Doing sums

1 Start a new page in your text editor. Type in this code:

```
Text editor
<script>
    document.write(10+10);
</script>
```

Save your file as **numbers.html** then double-click it to test it.

numbers.html

2 Arrange your desktop so you have your text editor on the left of the screen and your web browser on the right.

Semi-colon at end of the JavaScript

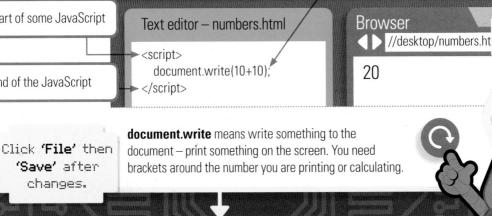

The start of some JavaScript

The end of the JavaScript

```
Text editor – numbers.html
<script>
    document.write(10+10);
</script>
```

```
Browser
◀ ▶ //desktop/numbers.ht
20
```

Refresh!

Click **'File'** then **'Save'** after changes.

document.write means write something to the document – print something on the screen. You need brackets around the number you are printing or calculating.

Now try these

50+40
80-25

Type in these code examples. Save and refresh your page each time to test. Answers are on page 122.

1
```
Text editor – numbers.html
<script>
    document.write(50+40);
</script>
```

2
```
Text editor – numbers.html
<script>
    document.write(80-25);
</script>
```

Answers are on page 122.

Key word

Loop: A sequence of commands repeated a number of times.

Loops and repeating

We can use loops to write something on the screen over and over again by using a 'for' loop.

Edit your code so it says:

Check you have typed the code carefully. It should display 123456789.

Text editor – numbers.html

```
<script>
  for(var n=1; n<10; n++)
    document.write(n);
</script>
```

Save and refresh to test!

numbers.html

Key word

Variable: A value or piece of data stored by a computer program.

How does it work?

var means variable. | **n** starts at 1. | **n** stops before 10. | **n++** makes n get bigger.

```
for(var n=1; n<10; n++)
  document.write(n);
```

This makes a loop using a variable called **n** that starts at 1. It goes up by 1 each loop and writes the value of n on the document. It keeps looping until n gets to 10.

Then try these

Type in these code examples. We are going to use **writeln(n)** rather than **write(n)** to leave a gap between each number. Answers are on page 122.

Make sure you get the semi-colons in the right places!

3 **Text editor – numbers.html**

```
<script>
  for(var n=10; n<20; n++)
    document.writeln(n);
</script>
```

4 **Text editor – numbers.html**

```
<script>
  for(var n=20; n<40; n++)
    document.writeln(n);
</script>
```

5 **Text editor – numbers.html**

```
<script>
  for(var n=1; n<10; n++)
    document.writeln(10-n);
</script>
```

6 **Text editor – numbers.html**

```
<script>
  for(var n=20; n>0; n--)
    document.writeln(n);
</script>
```

7 Make a loop that counts from 1 to 100.   **8** Make a loop that counts from 1 to 1000.

JAVASCRIPT FUNCTIONS

Key word

Input: An action (such as pressing a key) that tells a program to do something.

We've seen how we can use loops to repeat lines of code using JavaScript. However, there are times when we just want to repeat some parts of our code again, using different values. To do this, we need to create our own commands called functions.

Make a sandwich

In order to understand the idea of functions, imagine you need to teach a robot how to make sandwiches. You could give it instructions on how to make a cheese and pickle sandwich, then another set of instructions on how to make an egg and cress sandwich... and so on. You would end up writing lots of instructions.

I can make any sandwich now! What do you fancy?

I'm never going to remember all this!

...os and Bean Sandwich:
...bread.
Butter the bread.
Put humou... ...top of it.
...ut beans ...
Put the ot...
Cut the s...

To Make an...
Get two slice...
Butter the...
Put egg on...
Put cress on top of tha...
Put the other slice on top.
Cut the sandwich.

To Make a Cheese and Pickle S...
Get two slices of bread.
Butter the bread.
Put cheese on top of it.
Put pickle on top...
Put the oth...
Cut the s...

To Make a Cheese and Tomato Sandwich:
Get two slices of bread.
Butter the bread.
Put cheese on top of it.
Put tomato on top of that.
Put the other slice on top.
Cut the sandwich.

To Make a Sandwich With (filling1, filling2):
Get two slices of bread.
Butter the bread.
Put **filling1** on top of it.
Put **filling2** on top of that.
Put the other slice on top.
Cut the sandwich.

Instead we could tell our robot how to make any sandwich. Since we don't know what fillings we will need, we will just name them 'filling1' and 'filling2'. We will then write a general sandwich instruction that can be used over and over again, like a function.

NOW INSTEAD OF SAYING:

Make a cheese and tomato sandwich

Make a humous and bean sandwich

...WE WOULD NEED TO SAY:

Make a sandwich with ("cheese", "tomato").

Make a sandwich with ("humous", "bean").

Make a quiz

We are going to make a quiz program. We need to write code to ask a question, then check if it is correct or not, then tell the player. It could look like this:

```
<script>
  var answer=prompt("What is 5 x 5?");
  if(answer=="25") alert("Well done");
  else alert("Wrong");

  var answer=prompt("What is 10 x 10?");
  if(answer=="100") alert("Well done");
  else alert("Wrong");

  var answer=prompt("What is 3 x 3?");
  if(answer=="9") alert("Well done");
  else alert("Wrong");
</script>
```

Key word

Function: A sequence of commands that performs a specific task every time the function is 'called'.

This line asks for an input and stores the response in a variable called **answer**.

This checks whether the answer is correct and shows 'Well Done' if it is.

If the answer is not correct, it shows 'Wrong'.

This works but each question needs 3 lines of code. We need a quicker way!

Instead of repeating 3 lines of code for each question, we can create a function called **ask**. The function will be 'called' (run) every time we want to ask a question.

Type the curly brackets correctly: { and }.

```
<script>
  function ask(question, correct){
    var answer=prompt(question);
    if(answer==correct) alert("Well done");
    else alert("Wrong");
  }

  ask("what is 5 x 5","25");
  ask("what is 10 x 10","100");
  ask("what is 3 x 3","9");
</script>
```

This line starts defining the **ask** function.

The function uses similar code to before, but instead of using words like 'What is 3 x 3?' it uses a variable called **question**.

These lines ask the questions. They 'call' the function and pass it values to use as each question and answer.

1 Start a new page in your text editor. Type in the JavaScript code above.

2 Save your file as **quiz.html** then double-click it to test it.

3 Now add more questions of your own using the **ask** function.

JS FUNCTIONS WITH HTML

We've seen how JavaScript functions can be used to code a simple linear program. 'Linear' means the functions run one after another. We are now going to learn to make different functions run when different buttons are clicked.

Changing colour

We are going to make a web page that can change colour when different buttons are clicked. To start with, we are going to make a page with a button on it, and a function to change the page colour. Finally we will make the function run when the button is clicked.

1 Start a new web page in your text editor. Type in this JavaScript:

Text editor

```
<script>
  function red(){
    document.body.style.backgroundColor="red";
  }
</script>
```

2 Save your file as **change.html** then double-click it to test it so far.

3 Arrange your desktop so you have your text editor on the left of the screen and your web browser on the right.

Text editor – change.html

```
<script>
  function red(){
    document.body.style.backgroundColor="red";
  }
</script>
```

Browser

Refresh

4 Edit your file:

Add an **<html>** tag.

Add a button that will call the **red()** function.

Add an **</html>** tag.

Text editor – change.html

```
<html>
  <button onclick="red()">Go red</button>
  <script>
    function red(){
      document.body.style.backgroundColor="red";
    }
  </script>
</html>
```

5 Save and test your file. Click the **'Go red'** button and the page should change!

More colours, more functions?

It would be great if we could add lots more buttons to change the page to other colours. But that would mean adding a separate function for each colour. Instead we could make a general 'change background colour' function named **setbg**. We could 'pass' it a colour like we passed fillings to the sandwich function on page 112.

We would 'call' (run) the function like this: **setbg('red')** or **setbg('blue')** and so on.

Add an **<html>** tag.

Add a **button** that will call the **setbg()** function.

Add an **</html>** tag.

Go blue   Go green

Try adding more buttons to change to other colours...

Remember to type everything carefully. You need to spell colour the American way: color!

① Start a new web page in your text editor. Type in:

Text editor

```
<script>
  function setbg(col){
    document.body.style.backgroundColor=col;
  }
</script>
```

② Edit your file:

Text editor

```
<html>
<button onclick="setbg('blue')">Go blue</button>
<script>
  function setbg(col){
    document.body.style.backgroundColor=col;
  }
</script>
</html>
```

③ Save your file as **colours.html** then double-click it to test it so far.

④ Edit your file:

Text editor – colours.html

```
<html>
<button onclick="setbg('blue')">Go blue</button>
<button onclick="setbg('green')">Go green</button>
<script>
  function setbg(col){
    document.body.style.backgroundColor=col;
  }
</script>
</html>
```

Insert a new **button** here. Make it call the **setbg()** function.

⑤ Save and test your file. Click the buttons and the page should change colour!

PETS PROJECT

Most websites have more than one page. Each page is linked together so anyone using the site can move from page to page. We are going to make a simple site with pages about different animals. We will only be using HTML.

1 Start a new web page in your text editor. Type in this HTML:

Text editor

```
<html>
  <h1>Animals</h1>
</html>
```

2 Make a new folder for your project called **'Animals'**. Save your file in it, calling it **index.html**.

3 Open the **Animals** folder and double-click the **index.html** file to test it.

index.html

4 Arrange your desktop so you have the Animals folder, your text editor and your browser all visible at once.

Text editor – index.html

```
<html>
  <h1>Animals</h1>
</html>
```

Browser

//desktop/Animals/index.html

Animals

Files: desktop/Animals

index.html

To make a new folder on a Mac, click **'File'**, **'Save'** and **'New Folder'**.

On a PC, right-click in the **Save** box, click **'New'** and **'Folder'**.

5 In your text editor, click **'File'** and **'New'** to start the next page. Type in this HTML:

```
<html>
  <h1>Dogs</h1>
</html>
```

Save this one as **dogs.html** in the **Animals** folder.

Files: desktop/Animals

dogs.html

index.html

We now have two pages. The next task is to link these pages together. For a reminder about making links, see pages 104 and 105.

6 Edit your **index.html** file by adding a link to the **dogs.html** page:

Text editor – index.html
```
<html>
 <h1>Animals</h1>
 <a href="dogs.html">Dogs</a>
</html>
```

7 Refresh the page:

Browser `//desktop/Animals/index`

Animals
<u>Dogs</u>

Click the **'Dogs'** link...

Browser `//desktop/Animals/dogs`

Dogs

8 Repeat Step 5 to create another new file. Save it in the **Animals** folder as **cats.html**.

```
<html>
 <h1>Cats</h1>
</html>
```

9 Add another link to your **index.html** page to link it to the new **cats.html** page.

Add a **
** to make a line break and space out the links.

Text editor – index.html
```
<html>
 <h1>Animals</h1>
 <a href="dogs.html">Dogs</a>
 <br>
 <a href="cats.html">Cats</a>
</html>
```

10 Add more information about each animal on its page. Use **<p>** paragraph **</p>** tags around the information. Look back at page 107 to change the colours of pages and text.

Adding photos and pictures

To add photos or pictures to your Animals website, you could use your own digital photos of your pets. Alternatively, you can download pictures from the web. If you're going to display your website online, make sure you use photos that are not covered by copyright. If you're only going to show your website to classmates and family, you don't have to worry about copyright. For more information on copyright, see page 119.

Files: desktop/Animals

dogs.html   cats.html

Add your photo to the **Animals** folder.

Text editor – fish.html
```
<html>
 <h1>Fish</h1>
 <img src="fish.jpg">
</html>
```

Add an **<img>** (image) tag to display your photo.

Type the file name of the photo after **src =** and between double quotes. Src is short for source.

Browser `//desktop/Animals/fish.html`

Fish

117

SHARING YOUR WEBSITE

Once you have built a website or project on your computer, you may want to share it with other people. To do this you need to load it onto a special computer called a server, which can share it with the world. Make sure you get permission from a parent, carer or teacher first.

Website builders

There is lots of software to help people create their own websites, without having to do their own HTML coding. If you just want to make a website about a hobby, these easy-to-use 'website builders' are a good option – but you won't learn much about coding! If you search for 'website builders' you'll get a list of sites, some with free options. Make sure you ask an adult before you sign up.

1 HTML CONVENTIONS

In this chapter, we have used the shortest and simplest way to introduce you to HTML. Once you start sharing web pages, you need to follow standard conventions. Make sure all your pages have **<!DOCTYPE html>** at the start. Also include a title tag with the page title, for example: **<title>My web page</title>**. You should always include **<body>** tags (see page 107). Advanced coders include their style information in separate files (called CSS files) and their JavaScript in separate files, too. However, it is fine to use them within your HTML (called 'inline' to get started). For more information on web standards, visit: **http://www.w3.org**.

2 TEST YOUR SITE

Before you share your site, you need to test it to make sure it works properly on your computer. Read through your text and look for any spelling mistakes or missing punctuation marks. Ask a friend if they can use the site on your computer. Do the page titles and links make sense? Have you used colours that make the page easy to read?

3 E-SAFETY

If you are going to share your site on the web, anyone will be able to read it. Think carefully about any information or images you put on the pages, and always get permission from an adult. You should follow these rules, and any other rules about e-safety that you have at home and school:

- Don't share personal information – such as your full name, address or email address.
- Don't include photos of you or your family.
- Don't write anything unkind about other people on your site.

4 COPYRIGHT

Before you use photos or other images on your website, make sure you have permission to include them. If you download a photo from another website, make sure it is 'copyright free' or has been shared under a 'creative commons licence'. You should always credit the photographer.

You will be able to include a picture you have drawn in a painting program, or scanned onto your computer. If you have taken a photo of something (not someone!), then you will also be able to use it on your site.

5 WEBSPACE

You need to copy your website onto a special computer called a server that will host your website. The place to do this on the server is called webspace. You may have some free webspace provided as part of your internet or broadband access. If not, search online for 'webspace' or 'web hosting'. You can get free webspace or pay for your website to be hosted. You will need to pay more if you want a special website address. However, check with an adult before you do any of this.

6 UPLOADING

To upload your website, you need to use a special piece of software called an FTP program. FTP stands for File Transfer Protocol. It enables you to transfer the HTML files in your project folder from your computer to the server. You can download a free FTP program called FileZilla from **https://filezilla-project.org/**. See page 123 for more information.

You will need to enter login and password information from your web host.

Your website will now be live! Check it works OK. If there are any problems, fix them on your computer first, changing the files in your project folder. Then drag the files across to the remote site using the FTP program.

Drag files from the local folder to the remote folder on the right.

FTP

Local site:	desktop/Animals	Remote site:	public/www

cats.html

dogs.html

fish.html

index.html

fish.jpg

index.html

index.html

index.html

Browse your project folder on the left of the FTP program.

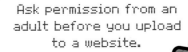

Ask permission from an adult before you upload to a website.

DEBUGGING

Coding can be a process of trial and error – testing ideas and seeing if they work. It is usual to make mistakes doing this. A bug is another name for a mistake in a piece of code that stops it working properly. Debugging means fixing those mistakes. Try these exercises then check your answers on page 122.

1

This HTML page needs to show each piece of fruit on a separate line...

Text editor – fruit.html

```
<html>
   <p>Apple</p>
   Banana
   Cranberry
   Date
</html>
```

...but it doesn't:

Browser

//desktop/fruit.html

Apple
Banana Cranberry Date

Debug it!

Debugging tips

When your code doesn't do what you want it to:

1. Check you have all the tags, colons, brackets and quotes you need and that they match.
2. Go through your code step by step, thinking about what each command and tag does.
3. Draw a picture or diagram to help.
4. Have a break for a few minutes!

2

This HTML should link to Google when it is clicked. But which version has no bugs: A, B, C or D? Why?

A
```
<html>
   <p>Click on a link:</p>
   <a href='http://www.google.com'>Google</a>
</html>
```

B
```
<html>
   <p>Click on a link:</p>
   <a href='Google'>http://www.google.com</a>
</html>
```

C
```
<html>
   <p>Click on a link:</p>
   <a href='http://www.google.com>Google</a>
</html>
```

D
```
<html>
   <p>Click on a link:</p>
   <a href='http://www.google.com'></a>Google
</html>
```

3

These HTML pages should colour the words 'Stop' and 'Go' in red and green, but all except one have bugs. Which one is correct: A, B, C or D? Why?

A
```html
<html>
    <p style='color:red'>Stop</p>
    <p style='color:green>Go</p>
</html>
```

B
```html
<html>
    <p style='color=red'>Stop</p>
    <p style='color=green'>Go</p>
</html>
```

C
```html
<html>
    <p style='color:red'>Stop</p>
    <p style='color:green'>Go</p>
</html>
```

D
```html
<html>
    <p color='red'>Stop</p>
    <p color='green'>Go</p>
</html>
```

4

This JavaScript should count from 1 all the way to 10...

Text editor – counting.html
```html
<script>
  for(var n=1; n<10; n++)
    document.writeln(n);
</script>
```

...but it doesn't:

Browser
◀▶ //desktop/counting.html ↻

1 2 3 4 5 6 7 8 9

Debug it!

Coding guidelines

Think about these guidelines when you are coding:

1 Plan your program carefully, either with a diagram or some notes.

2 When you are learning to code, it is better to write lots of small, simple programs rather than one larger and more complex program.

3 Test your program as you build it: don't wait until you have put all the commands in.

5

This JavaScript should count from 30 to 50...

...but it doesn't!

Text editor – numbers.html
```html
<script>
  for(var n=30; n<50; n++)
    document.writeln(30);
</script>
```

Browser
◀▶ //desktop/numbers.html ↻

30 30 30 30 30 30 30 30 30 30 30 30 30 30 30 30 30 30 30 30

Can you debug it?

CHAPTER 4 ANSWERS

Page 101

1

Browser
//desktop/headings

Cyber Cafe

Open every day

2

Browser
//desktop/headings

Code School

Smith Street

Learn to code

3

Browser
//desktop/headings

Huge

Medium

Tiny

4

Browser
//desktop/headings

London

England

Paris

France

Page 107

1

Browser
//desktop/styles.html

Tim Berners-Lee

Ada Lovelace

Alan Turing

2

Browser
//desktop/styles.html

Nelson Mandela

Mahatma Gandhi

Rosa Parks

Pages 110–111

1 90   **2** 55   **3** 10 11 12 13 14 15 16 17 18 19

4 20 21 22 23 ... 35 36 37 38 39   **5** 9 8 7 6 5 4 3 2 1

6 20 19 18 17 16 15 14 13 12 11 10 9 8 7 6 5 4 3 2 1

7

Text editor – numbers.html

```
<script>
  for(var n=1; n<101; n++)
    document.writeln(n);
</script>
```

8

Text editor – numbers.html

```
<script>
  for(var n=1; n<1001; n++)
    document.writeln(n);
</script>
```

Page 120–121

1 missing **<p>** and **</p>** tags around Banana, Cranberry and Date

2 Ⓐ correct

Ⓑ the URL and **'Google'** are switched round

Ⓒ missing quote after the URL

Ⓓ **</a>** should be after **Google**

3 Ⓐ missing quote after **green**

Ⓑ **'color=red'** should be **'color:red'**

Ⓒ correct

Ⓓ **color='red'** should be **style='color:red'**

4 **n<10** should be **n<11** or **n<=10**

5 two mistakes:
n<50 should be **n<=50** or **n<51**
document.writeln(30); should be
document.writeln(n);

TEXT EDITORS FOR HTML AND JAVASCRIPT

Before you start coding, you'll need a suitable text editor. Most computers will already have a text editor. On a PC, you'll find **Notepad**. On a Mac, you'll find **TextEdit**. These are fine for basic HTML.

SPECIALIST HTML EDITORS

If you intend to take your coding to the next level, you'll find that using a dedicated HTML editor will make things easier. A text editor that is designed to help you code in HTML will change the colour of your code to make it easier to check, and make sure you have all the tags typed properly. **Sublime Text** is a very useful text editor that you can download and try out for free. You will probably find Sublime Text useful for the activities from page 114 onwards. To download it, go to: **www.sublimetext.com**

FTP PROGRAMS

If you are going to upload HTML files to create a public website, you will need an FTP program to transfer the files. You can use **FileZilla** to do this for free. To download it, go to: **https://filezilla-project.org/.**

Choose to download the **'Client'** version, not the 'Server' version.

After downloading FileZilla, the first time you run it you will need to set it up. To do this you need to click **'File'** then **'Site manager'** and enter various bits of information. This will include username, password and the address of the site. This information should be provided by your web host.

ON A MAC: USING TEXTEDIT

If you are working with TextEdit, first of all click the **'TextEdit'** menu, then click **'Preferences'**.

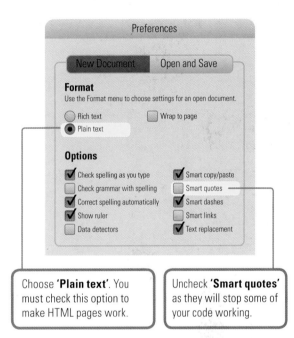

Choose **'Plain text'**. You must check this option to make HTML pages work.

Uncheck **'Smart quotes'** as they will stop some of your code working.

GLOSSARY

Algorithm A set of steps or rules to solve a problem.

Attribute Extra information about an object or text, such as its style, font, width or height.

Browser A program used to view websites and HTML pages. Popular browsers include Chrome, Firefox, Internet Explorer and Safari.

Code A set of words or blocks that tells a computer what to do.

Command A single word or code-block that tells the computer what to do.

Co-ordinates A set of numbers that gives the position of a point. It is common to use two numbers, called x and y. X gives the distance to the right or left of the screen. Y gives the distance up or down.

Data Information that can be stored and used by a computer.

Debugging Fixing problems (bugs) in a computer program.

Degree The unit of measurement for angles. If we turn all the way around, we turn 360 degrees. A quarter-turn is 90 degrees.

Download To copy data from one computer system to another, often using the internet.

Editor (or text editor) A program used to type and edit programs.

Email A system for sending messages from one computer to another using the internet.

Event Something that happens while a program is running, such as a key being pressed or a mouse button being clicked.

Function A sequence of commands created to do something such as draw a square every time the function is run or 'called'.

Graphics Data that is displayed as a picture, diagram or graph.

HTML (Hyper Text Mark-up Language) The language used to define the objects or elements that are on web pages.

HTTP (Hyper Text Transfer Protocol) Rules for transporting HTML pages over the internet.

Hyperlink Link to another web page, which can be reached by clicking the mouse or touching a touchscreen.

IDLE The editor used to write Python code.

If…then…else A common form of selection in coding, where a command is run if something is true, and a different command is run if it is false.

Import To take data from one program into another.

Input An action (like pressing a key) that tells a program to do something.

Integer A whole number, such as 1 or 24.

Internet A worldwide network of computers.

JavaScript The programming language used in some web pages to make them more interactive.

Language A system of words, numbers, symbols and rules for writing programs.

Library A collection of commands that are already stored and ready for use.

Listener A line of code or function that is only run when a particular event happens, such as a button being clicked.

Logo A computer language in which commands move a turtle around the screen to draw.

Loop A sequence of commands repeated a number of times.

Network A group of computers connected by wires or, often today, wireless links.

Online Connected to the internet.

Operator A piece of code that carries out a mathematical or logical operation.

Output Something that a computer program does to show the results of a program, such as moving a sprite or making a sound.

Pixel A unit of measurement used in computing. A pixel is the smallest dot you can see on your screen.

Processor The 'brain' of a computer. It carries out the instructions given by a computer program.

Program The special commands that tell a computer how to do something.

Protocol A system of rules.

Python A programming language that uses text (words, letters, numbers and keyboard symbols) to make a program.

Random When all possible choices have an equal chance of being picked.

Scratch A computer language that uses blocks to make programs.

Scripts area In Scratch, this is the area to the right of the Scratch screen, where you need to drag your code blocks to.

Selection The way a computer program chooses which commands to run, after a simple question or value check.

Server A computer or group of computers that stores and delivers web pages.

Sprite An object that moves around the screen.

Stage In Scratch, this is the area to the top left of the Scratch screen, where you can watch your sprites move about.

Tags Special words used to describe what objects there are on a web page. They are always surrounded by angle brackets <>.

Turtle A robot, sprite or arrow that can be programmed to move around the floor or the computer screen.

Upload To transfer files from your computer to another computer, which is often larger and in a different place.

URL (Uniform Resource Locator) The address or location of a website or HTML page. It is usually shown at the top of the browser window.

User The person using a program.

Variable A value or piece of data stored by a computer program.

Web page A page of information constructed using HTML and connected to the World Wide Web.

Wireless Communicating without connecting wires, often using radio waves.

World Wide Web (or web) A worldwide network of HTML files, which we can access using the internet.

INDEX

Browser

www.qed-publishing.co.uk/extra-resources.php